GRAMMAR
AND BEYOND

Randi Reppen
with Deborah Gordon

1A

CAMBRIDGE
UNIVERSITY PRESS

CAMBRIDGE
UNIVERSITY PRESS

32 Avenue of the Americas, New York, NY 10013-2473, USA

Cambridge University Press is part of the University of Cambridge.

It furthers the University's mission by disseminating knowledge in the pursuit of education, learning and research at the highest international levels of excellence.

www.cambridge.org
Information on this title: www.cambridge.org/9780521143042

© Cambridge University Press 2012

This publication is in copyright. Subject to statutory exception and to the provisions of relevant collective licensing agreements, no reproduction of any part may take place without the written permission of Cambridge University Press.

First published 2012
8th printing 2016

Printed in China by Golden Cup Printing Co. Ltd

A catalogue record for this publication is available from the British Library

ISBN 978-0-521-14293-9 Student's Book 1
ISBN 978-0-521-14304-2 Student's Book 1A
ISBN 978-0-521-14307-3 Student's Book 1B
ISBN 978-0-521-27988-8 Workbook 1
ISBN 978-0-521-27989-5 Workbook 1A
ISBN 978-0-521-27990-1 Workbook 1B
ISBN 978-1-107-69431-6 Teacher Support Resource Book with CD-ROM 1
ISBN 978-0-521-14330-1 Class Audio CD 1
ISBN 978-1-139-06183-4 Writing Skills Interactive 1

Cambridge University Press has no responsibility for the persistence or accuracy of URLs for external or third-party internet websites referred to in this publication, and does not guarantee that any content on such websites is, or will remain, accurate or appropriate. Information regarding prices, travel timetables, and other factual information given in this work is correct at the time of first printing but Cambridge University Press does not guarantee the accuracy of such information thereafter.

Book design and layout services: TSI Graphics
Art direction: Adventure House, NYC
Audio production: John Marshall Media

Contents

PART 1 The Verb *Be*

PART 2 Nouns, Determiners, and Pronouns

PART 6 **Simple Past**

PART 7A **More About Nouns and Determiners**

Appendices

Introduction to *Grammar and Beyond*

Grammar and Beyond is a research-based and content-rich grammar series for beginning- to advanced-level students of North American English. The series focuses on the grammar structures most commonly used in North American English, with an emphasis on the application of these grammar structures to academic writing. The series practices all four skills in a variety of authentic and communicative contexts. It is designed for use both in the classroom and as a self-study learning tool.

Grammar and Beyond Is Research-Based

The grammar presented in this series is informed by years of research on the grammar of written and spoken North American English as it is used in college lectures, textbooks, academic essays, high school classrooms, and conversations between instructors and students. This research, and the analysis of over one billion words of authentic written and spoken language data known as the *Cambridge International Corpus*, has enabled the authors to:

- Present grammar rules that accurately represent how North American English is actually spoken and written

- Identify and teach differences between the grammar of written and spoken English

- Focus more attention on the structures that are commonly used, and less attention on those that are rarely used, in written and spoken North American English

- Help students avoid the most common mistakes that English language learners make

- Choose reading and writing topics that will naturally elicit examples of the target grammar structure

- Introduce important vocabulary from the Academic Word List

Grammar and Beyond Teaches Academic Writing Skills

Grammar and Beyond helps students make the transition from understanding grammar structures to applying them in their academic writing.

In the Student's Books

At Levels 1 through 3 of the series, every Student's Book unit ends with a section devoted to the hands-on application of grammar to writing. This section, called Grammar for Writing, explores how and where the target grammar structures function in writing and offers controlled practice, exposure to writing models, and a guided but open-ended writing task.

At Level 4, the most advanced level, the syllabus is organized around the academic essay types that college students write (e.g., persuasive, cause and effect) and is aimed at teaching students the grammar, vocabulary, and writing skills that they need in order to be successful at writing those kinds of essays.

Online

Grammar and Beyond also offers *Writing Skills Interactive*, an interactive online course in academic writing skills and vocabulary that correlates with the Student's Books. Each unit of the writing skills course focuses on a specific writing skill, such as avoiding sentence fragments or developing strong topic sentences.

Special Features of *Grammar and Beyond*

Realistic Grammar Presentations

Grammar is presented in clear and simple charts. The grammar points presented in these charts have been tested against real-world data from the *Cambridge International Corpus* to ensure that they are authentic representations of actual use of North American English.

Data from the Real World

Many of the grammar presentations and application sections in the Student's Book include a feature called Data from the Real World, in which concrete and useful points discovered through analysis of corpus data are presented. These points are practiced in the exercises that follow.

Avoid Common Mistakes

Each Student's Book unit features an Avoid Common Mistakes section that develops students' awareness of the most common mistakes made by English language learners and gives them an opportunity to practice detecting and correcting these errors in running text. This section helps students avoid these mistakes in their own work. The mistakes highlighted in this section are drawn from a body of authentic data on learner English known as the *Cambridge Learner Corpus*, a database of over 35 million words from student essays written by nonnative speakers of English and information from experienced classroom teachers.

Academic Vocabulary

Every unit in *Grammar and Beyond* includes words from the Academic Word List (AWL), a research-based list of words and word families that appear with high frequency in English-language academic texts. These words are introduced in the opening text of the unit, recycled in the charts and exercises, and used to support the theme throughout the unit. The same vocabulary items are reviewed and practiced in *Writing Skills Interactive*, the online writing skills course. By the time students finish each level, they will have been exposed several times to a carefully selected set of level-appropriate AWL words, as well as content words from a variety of academic disciplines.

Series Levels

The following table provides a general idea of the difficulty of the material at each level of *Grammar and Beyond*. These are not meant to be interpreted as precise correlations.

	Description	TOEFL IBT	CEFR Levels
Level 1	beginning	20 – 34	A1 – A2
Level 2	low intermediate to intermediate	35 – 54	A2 – B1
Level 3	high intermediate	55 – 74	B1 – B2
Level 4	advanced	75 – 95	B2 – C1

Components for Students

Student's Book

The Student's Books for Levels 1 through 3 teach all of the grammar points appropriate at each level in short, manageable cycles of presentation and practice organized around a high-interest unit theme. The Level 4 Student's Book focuses on the structure of the academic essay in addition to the grammar rules, conventions, and structures that students need to master in order to be successful college writers. Please see the Tour of a Unit on pages xvi–xix for a more detailed view of the contents and structure of the Student's Book units.

Workbook

The Workbook provides additional practice of the grammar presented in each unit of the Student's Book. The exercises offer both discrete and consolidated practice of grammar points and can be used for homework or in class. Each unit also offers practice correcting the errors highlighted in the Avoid Common Mistakes section in the Student's Book to help students master these troublesome errors. Self-Assessment sections at the end of each unit allow students to test their mastery of what they have learned.

Writing Skills Interactive

This online course provides graduated instruction and practice in writing skills, while reinforcing vocabulary presented in the Student's Books. Each unit includes a vocabulary review activity, followed by a short text that builds on the theme presented in the Student's Book and provides an additional context for the vocabulary. The text is followed by an animated interactive presentation of the target writing skill of the unit, after which students have the opportunity to practice the target skill in three different activities. Each unit closes with a quiz, which allows students to assess their progress.

Teacher Resources

Teacher Support Resource Book with CD-ROM

This comprehensive book provides a range of support materials for instructors, including:

- Suggestions for applying the target grammar to all four major skill areas, helping instructors facilitate dynamic and comprehensive grammar classes
- An answer key and audio script for the Student's Book
- A CD-ROM containing:
  - Ready-made, easily scored Unit Tests
  - PowerPoint presentations to streamline lesson preparation and encourage lively heads-up interaction

Class Audio CD

The class audio CD for each level provides the Student's Book listening material for in-class use.

Teacher Support Website

www.cambridge.org/grammarandbeyond

The website for *Grammar and Beyond* contains even more resources for instructors, including:

- Unit-by-unit teaching tips, helping instructors plan their lessons
- Downloadable communicative activities to add more in-class speaking practice
- A monthly newsletter on grammar teaching, providing ongoing professional development

We hope you enjoy using this series, and we welcome your feedback! Please send any comments to the authors and editorial staff at Cambridge University Press, at grammarandbeyond@cambridge.org.

About the Authors

Randi Reppen is Professor of Applied Linguistics and TESL at Northern Arizona University (NAU) in Flagstaff, Arizona. She has over 20 years experience teaching ESL students and training ESL teachers, including 11 years as the Director of NAU's Program in Intensive English. Randi's research interests focus on the use of corpora for language teaching and materials development. In addition to numerous academic articles and books, she is the author of *Using Corpora in the Language Classroom* and a co-author of *Basic Vocabulary in Use*, 2nd edition, both published by Cambridge University Press.

Deborah Gordon, creator of the Grammar for Writing sections, has more than 25 years' experience teaching ESL students and training ESL teachers in the United States and abroad. She is currently an ESL instructor at Santa Barbara City College and a TESOL Certificate instructor at the University of California, Santa Barbara Extension. Deborah is coauthor of *Writers at Work: From Sentence to Paragraph*, published by Cambridge University Press, among many other titles.

Corpus Consultants

Michael McCarthy is Emeritus Professor of Applied Linguistics at the University of Nottingham, UK, and Adjunct Professor of Applied Linguistics at the Pennsylvania State University. He is a co-author of the corpus-informed *Touchstone* series and the award-winning *Cambridge Grammar of English*, both published by Cambridge University Press, among many other titles, and is known throughout the world as an expert on grammar, vocabulary, and corpus linguistics.

Jeanne McCarten has over 30 years of experience in ELT/ESL as a teacher, publisher, and author. She has been closely involved in the development of the spoken English sections of the *Cambridge International Corpus*. Now a freelance writer, she is co-author of the corpus-informed *Touchstone* series and *Grammar for Business*, both published by Cambridge University Press.

Advisory Panel

The ESL advisory panel has helped to guide the development of this series and provided invaluable information about the needs of ESL students and teachers in high schools, colleges, universities, and private language schools throughout North America.

Neta Simpkins Cahill, Skagit Valley College, Mount Vernon, WA

Shelly Hedstrom, Palm Beach State College, Lake Worth, FL

Richard Morasci, Foothill College, Los Altos Hills, CA

Stacey Russo, East Hampton High School, East Hampton, NY

Alice Savage, North Harris College, Houston, TX

Acknowledgments

The publisher and authors would like to thank these reviewers and consultants for their insights and participation:

Marty Attiyeh, The College of DuPage, Glen Ellyn, IL

Shannon Bailey, Austin Community College, Austin, TX

Jamila Barton, North Seattle Community College, Seattle, WA

Kim Bayer, Hunter College IELI, New York, NY

Linda Berendsen, Oakton Community College, Skokie, IL

Anita Biber, Tarrant County College Northwest, Fort Worth, TX

Jane Breaux, Community College of Aurora, Aurora, CO

Anna Budzinski, San Antonio College, San Antonio, TX

Britta Burton, Mission College, Santa Clara, CA

Jean Carroll, Fresno City College, Fresno, CA

Chris Cashman, Oak Park High School and Elmwood Park High School, Chicago, IL

Annette M. Charron, Bakersfield College, Bakersfield, CA

Patrick Colabucci, ALI at San Diego State University, San Diego, CA

Lin Cui, Harper College, Palatine, IL

Jennifer Duclos, Boston University CELOP, Boston, MA

Joy Durighello, San Francisco City College, San Francisco, CA

Kathleen Flynn, Glendale Community College, Glendale, CA

Raquel Fundora, Miami Dade College, Miami, FL

Patricia Gillie, New Trier Township High School District, Winnetka, IL

Laurie Gluck, LaGuardia Community College, Long Island City, NY

Kathleen Golata, Galileo Academy of Science & Technology, San Francisco, CA

Ellen Goldman, Mission College, Santa Clara, CA

Ekaterina Goussakova, Seminole Community College, Sanford, FL

Marianne Grayston, Prince George's Community College, Largo, MD

Mary Greiss Shipley, Georgia Gwinnett College, Lawrenceville, GA

Sudeepa Gulati, Long Beach City College, Long Beach, CA

Nicole Hammond Carrasquel, University of Central Florida, Orlando, FL

Vicki Hendricks, Broward College, Fort Lauderdale, FL

Kelly Hernandez, Miami Dade College, Miami, FL

Ann Johnston, Tidewater Community College, Virginia Beach, VA

Julia Karet, Chaffey College, Claremont, CA

Jeanne Lachowski, English Language Institute, University of Utah, Salt Lake City, UT

Noga Laor, Rennert, New York, NY

Min Lu, Central Florida Community College, Ocala, FL

Michael Luchuk, Kaplan International Centers, New York, NY

Craig Machado, Norwalk Community College, Norwalk, CT

Denise Maduli-Williams, City College of San Francisco, San Francisco, CA

Diane Mahin, University of Miami, Coral Gables, FL

Melanie Majeski, Naugatuck Valley Community College, Waterbury, CT

Jeanne Malcolm, University of North Carolina at Charlotte, Charlotte, NC

Lourdes Marx, Palm Beach State College, Boca Raton, FL

Susan G. McFalls, Maryville College, Maryville, TN

Nancy McKay, Cuyahoga Community College, Cleveland, OH

Dominika McPartland, Long Island Business Institute, Flushing, NY

Amy Metcalf, UNR/Intensive English Language Center, University of Nevada, Reno, NV

Robert Miller, EF International Language School San Francisco – Mills, San Francisco, CA

Marcie Pachino, Jordan High School, Durham, NC

Myshie Pagel, El Paso Community College, El Paso, TX

Bernadette Pedagno, University of San Francisco, San Francisco, CA

Tam Q Pham, Dallas Theological Seminary, Fort Smith, AR

Mary Beth Pickett, Global-LT, Rochester, MI

Maria Reamore, Baltimore City Public Schools, Baltimore, MD

Alison M. Rice, Hunter College IELI, New York, NY

Sydney Rice, Imperial Valley College, Imperial, CA

Kathleen Romstedt, Ohio State University, Columbus, OH

Alexandra Rowe, University of South Carolina, Columbia, SC

Irma Sanders, Baldwin Park Adult and Community Education, Baldwin Park, CA

Caren Shoup, Lone Star College – CyFair, Cypress, TX

Karen Sid, Mission College, Foothill College, De Anza College, Santa Clara, CA

Michelle Thomas, Miami Dade College, Miami, FL

Sharon Van Houte, Lorain County Community College, Elyria, OH

Margi Wald, UC Berkeley, Berkeley, CA

Walli Weitz, Riverside County Office of Ed., Indio, CA

Bart Weyand, University of Southern Maine, Portland, ME

Donna Weyrich, Columbus State Community College, Columbus, OH

Marilyn Whitehorse, Santa Barbara City College, Ojai, CA

Jessica Wilson, Rutgers University – Newark, Newark, NJ

Sue Wilson, San Jose City College, San Jose, CA

Margaret Wilster, Mid-Florida Tech, Orlando, FL

Anne York-Herjeczki, Santa Monica College, Santa Monica, CA

Hoda Zaki, Camden County College, Camden, NJ

We would also like to thank these teachers and programs for allowing us to visit:

Richard Appelbaum, Broward College, Fort Lauderdale, FL

Carmela Arnoldt, Glendale Community College, Glendale, AZ

JaNae Barrow, Desert Vista High School, Phoenix, AZ

Ted Christensen, Mesa Community College, Mesa, AZ

Richard Ciriello, Lower East Side Preparatory High School, New York, NY

Virginia Edwards, Chandler-Gilbert Community College, Chandler, AZ

Nusia Frankel, Miami Dade College, Miami, FL

Raquel Fundora, Miami Dade College, Miami, FL

Vicki Hendricks, Broward College, Fort Lauderdale, FL

Kelly Hernandez, Miami Dade College, Miami, FL

Stephen Johnson, Miami Dade College, Miami, FL

Barbara Jordan, Mesa Community College, Mesa, AZ

Nancy Kersten, GateWay Community College, Phoenix, AZ

Lewis Levine, Hostos Community College, Bronx, NY

John Liffiton, Scottsdale Community College, Scottsdale, AZ

Cheryl Lira-Layne, Gilbert Public School District, Gilbert, AZ

Mary Livingston, Arizona State University, Tempe, AZ

Elizabeth Macdonald, Thunderbird School of Global Management, Glendale, AZ

Terri Martinez, Mesa Community College, Mesa, AZ

Lourdes Marx, Palm Beach State College, Boca Raton, FL

Paul Kei Matsuda, Arizona State University, Tempe, AZ

David Miller, Glendale Community College, Glendale, AZ

Martha Polin, Lower East Side Preparatory High School, New York, NY

Patricia Pullenza, Mesa Community College, Mesa, AZ

Victoria Rasinskaya, Lower East Side Preparatory High School, New York, NY

Vanda Salls, Tempe Union High School District, Tempe, AZ

Kim Sanabria, Hostos Community College, Bronx, NY

Cynthia Schuemann, Miami Dade College, Miami, FL

Michelle Thomas, Miami Dade College, Miami, FL

Dongmei Zeng, Borough of Manhattan Community College, New York, NY

Tour of a Unit

UNIT

11

Conjunctions: *And, But, Or; Because*
Time Management

1 Grammar in the Real World

A Do you have enough time for school, work, and family? Read the article below. What is one way to manage your time well?

Time for Everything

Many adults say they want more time. They are busy with work, family, **and** school, **and** they often don't get everything done. People feel stressed **because** there is not enough time to do it all. However, there are some simple ways to manage your time well **and** avoid stress.

One way is to identify the important **or** necessary tasks for that day. Then create a schedule **or** a "to do" list.[1] When you finish your important tasks, you can move on to the next, less important ones. Soon your tasks are done, **and** there is hopefully some extra time for fun activities.

Another way is to do important tasks on the same days every week. For example, you can do your laundry every Monday, **and** go to the gym on Tuesday and Thursday mornings before work or school. Always do the tasks on the same days. That way, you can plan around these important tasks **and** have time for other things. Some people don't like schedules, lists, or weekly plans. Instead, they use the notes or calendar features on their cell phones. Put a reminder[2] for the task on your phone, **but** don't forget to do it!

These ideas can help you improve your time management.[3] When you make plans and complete them, you feel good **and** can do more.

To Do:
grocery shopping
laundry
walk the dog

Monday	Tuesday
7:00 laundry	8:00 gym
9:00 work	10:00 class

[1] **"to do" list:** a list of things you need to do | [2] **reminder:** something that helps someone remember, like an alarm on a phone | [3] **time management:** being in control of your time; planning and using your time well

122

B *Comprehension Check* Answer the questions. Use the article to help you.

1. What do most adults not have enough of?
2. What are two ways to manage your time?
3. What happens when people make plans and complete them?

C *Notice* Find the words *and, but, or,* and *because* in the article. Then complete the sentences.

1. They are busy with work, family, _____ school.
2. People feel stressed _____ there is not enough time to do it all.
3. Some people don't like schedules, lists, _____ weekly plans.
4. Put a reminder for the task on your phone, _____ don't forget to do it!

2 And, But, Or

▶ Grammar Presentation

And, but, and *or* are coordinating conjunctions. They connect words, phrases, and clauses.

People are busy with family **and** work.
I like to exercise, **but** I don't have time for it every day.
She studies in the morning **or** after work.

2.1 *And, But, Or* for Connecting Words and Phrases

Connecting Words	*Time and money* are valuable. She sleeps only *five or six* hours a night.
Connecting Phrases	I always *make a schedule and look at it often.* I have "to do" lists *on my computer but not on my phone.* Do you work *during the day or at night*?

2.2 *And, But, Or* for Connecting Clauses

First Clause		Second Clause
You have more time in your day,	**and**	you feel less stressed.
Some people use their time well,	**but**	other people do not.
You can make a list,	**or**	you can schedule tasks on the same days.

2.3 Using *And, But, Or*

a. Use *and*, *but*, and *or* to connect words, phrases, and clauses.	Time **and** money are valuable. He has time **but** not money. Do you use schedules, **or** do you make "to do" lists?
b. Use *and* to join two or more ideas.	Maria makes time for school, family, **and** work. I study **and** work every day. I make a "to do" list, **and** I check the list often during the day.
c. Use *but* to show contrast or surprising information.	José works hard, **but** he also has fun. He always makes a schedule, **but** he rarely follows it.
d. Use *or* to show a choice of two alternatives.	You can make lists **or** schedules. I exercise **or** do laundry after I study. Is he at school **or** at work?
e. Use a comma when *and*, *but*, and *or* connect two clauses.	My family gets together at night, **and** we talk about our day. Sonya wakes up early, **but** she is always late for work.

▶ **Grammar Application**

Exercise 2.1 Choosing *And, But, Or*

A Read the sentences about two types of people. Complete the sentences with *and, but,* or *or.* Add commas where necessary.

The Organized Person

1. Every day I wake up, *and* I make a long "to do" list.
2. I usually use the "notes" feature on my phone for important tasks _____ I always do them.
3. I don't like to forget appointments _____ be late.
4. I like to be busy _____ I feel good when I get things done.

The Disorganized Person

5. Sometimes I make lists _____ I usually lose them.
6. I have a lot of appointments _____ a lot of things to do every day.
7. I try to be on time _____ I am often late for appointments.
8. I am always busy _____ I don't get things done.

B *Over to You* Read the sentences in A with a partner. Which statements are true for you? Tell your partner.

Exercise 2.4 Vocabulary Focus: Expressions with *And* and *Or*

Data from the Real World

English has many expressions using *and* and *or.* The nouns usually occur in the order they appear below.	Do you like peanut butter and jelly? NOT ~~Do you like jelly and peanut butter?~~	
Common "noun *and* noun" expressions for food	cream **and** sugar salt **and** pepper bread **and** butter	peanut butter **and** jelly fish **and** chips
Common "noun *and* noun" expressions for relationships	mom **and** dad brother **and** sister husband **and** wife	Mr. **and** Mrs. father **and** son mother **and** daughter
Other common "noun *and* noun" expressions	night **and** day men **and** women name **and** address	ladies **and** gentlemen boys **and** girls
Common expressions with *or*	cash **or** credit	coffee **or** tea
Common "adjective *and* adjective" expressions	black **and** white old **and** new	nice **and** warm

A Complete the questions.

1. Do you like *cream* and sugar with your coffee?
2. Do your _____ and dad live in the United States?
3. Do you have brothers and _____ ?
4. Do you work _____ and day?
5. Do you like black and _____ movies?
6. Do you think _____ and women have really different interests?
7. Do you put salt and _____ on your food?
8. Do you usually pay with _____ or credit?
9. Do you ever eat peanut butter and _____ sandwiches?
10. Do you prefer _____ or tea?

A **wide variety** of exercises introduce new and stimulating content to keep students engaged with the material.

Students learn to *Avoid Common Mistakes* based on research in student writing.

▶ Grammar Application

Exercise 3.1 Cause-and-Effect Relationships with *Because*

Match the effect on the left with the cause on the right.

1. John is tired ___c___
2. Tanya is usually late _____
3. Dan is often hungry _____
4. Eric walks slowly _____
5. Sue takes her brother to school _____
6. Maya and Sara sleep late _____
7. Jack takes classes at night _____

a. because his foot hurts.
b. because he never eats breakfast.
c. because he doesn't sleep enough.
d. because he works during the day.
e. because she doesn't put reminders on her phone.
f. because their mother doesn't have time.
g. because their alarm clocks don't work.

Exercise 3.2 ◀)) The Position of *Because*

Put *because* in the correct place in each sentence. Add commas where necessary. Then listen and compare your answers.

Bob, Jamal, Tony, and Leo are roommates. They study at the local community college. Each roommate has a problem with time.

                    because
1. Leo works at night he goes to school during the day.
2. Tony can only study in the mornings he thinks more clearly then.
3. Bob's alarm clock doesn't work he is always late.
4. Jamal can't study at home his roommates are too noisy.
5. Leo forgets to write his assignments down he often misses them.
6. Tony and Jamal sometimes miss class they play basketball instead.

4 Avoid Common Mistakes ⚠

1. **Do not use a comma when you join two words or two phrases.**
   Lisa creates a schedule, and a list every day.
2. **Use a comma when you join two clauses with *and*, *but*, and *or*.**
   I need to study for the test and then I have to work!
3. **Use *and* to add information. Use *but* to show a contrast. Use *or* to show a choice.**
                                  but
   Sam is always late, and he gets his work done.
4. **Do not use a comma if *because* is in the second part of the sentence.**
   Jake is always on time, because he takes the 8:00 bus to school every day.

   But do use a comma if *because* is in the first part of the sentence.
   Because Lily makes a daily schedule she never forgets to do her tasks.
5. **Use *because* to state the reason (cause) for something. The other part of the sentence states the result (effect).**
   Because Kylie writes her assignments on her calendar,
   Kylie writes her assignments on her calendar because she doesn't forget them.
   Kylie doesn't forget her assignments because
   Because Kylie doesn't forget her assignments, she writes them on her calendar.

Editing Task

Read the story about Professor Kwan's class on time management. Find and correct 9 more mistakes.

A Useful Class

Every year, Professor Kwan teaches a class on time management. Many students like to take her class. Sometimes the class fills up quickly/because it is so popular. Students know that they need to register early – in person and online. This is the first lesson of the time-management class.

5   In this class, Professor Kwan talks about different ways for students to organize their time. Her students often complain about the stress they have but how little

After studying what **common mistakes** to avoid, students apply the information in **editing tasks**.

Grammar for Writing connects the unit's grammar to specific **applications** in writing.

The final writing exercise **brings everything together** as students apply their knowledge of the unit's grammar in a level-appropriate **writing task**.

5 Grammar for Writing

Describing the Way You Do Something

Writers use *and, but, or,* and *because* to combine ideas and to show relationships between ideas. They can use these conjunctions to write about something they do regularly.
Remember:

- **Use *and, but, or* or to combine words, phrases, or clauses.**
  I usually do my homework on the bus <u>and</u> on my lunch break.
  She does her homework at night, <u>but</u> sometimes she falls asleep.
  His homework is never late <u>or</u> incomplete.

- **Use *because* to show a cause-and-effect relationship between two sentences.**
  She has very little time <u>because</u> she has two jobs.

Pre-writing Task

1 Read the paragraph below. When and where does the writer do her homework? Why?

Doing My Homework

I'm always busy (because) I work and I take classes.
I don't have a lot of time for homework because of this.
Because my homework is important, I do it in the library
before or after my class. The library opens at 7:00 a.m.,
5 and my class starts at 8:00 a.m. The library is quiet at
7:00 a.m. because it is often empty then. Sometimes I ask
the librarians for help. They are usually very nice and
helpful, but sometimes they are busy with their work.
After class, the library is full, but it is still a good place
10 to study.

2 Read the paragraph again. Circle the conjunctions *and, but, or,* and *because.* Which conjunctions connect words? Which connect phrases? Which connect clauses?

Writing Task

1 *Write* Use the paragraph in the Pre-writing Task to help you write about something you need to do regularly. Do you schedule time for this activity? When and where do you do this activity? Explain why. Write about how you:

- clean house
- do dishes
- do homework
- do laundry
- exercise
- go food shopping
- make meals
- pay bills
- take care of children

Use *and, but, or,* and *because* to combine ideas and show relationships between ideas.

2 *Self-Edit* Use the editing tips below to improve your sentences. Make any necessary changes.

1. Did you use conjunctions to write about something you do regularly?
2. Did you use *and, but,* and *or* to connect words, phrases, or clauses?
3. Did you use *because* to show cause-and-effect relationships?
4. Did you avoid the mistakes in the Avoid Common Mistakes chart on page 130?

A **Pre-writing Task** uses a model to guide students' **analysis** of grammar in **writing**.

UNIT 1

Statements with Present of *Be*

Tell Me About Yourself

1 | Grammar in the Real World

A How do you introduce yourself to your instructors? What information do you give? Read the conversation between an adviser and a student. What are two interesting facts about Jun-Ho?

First Meeting with an Adviser

Jun-Ho	Hello, Mr. Garcia. I'**m** Jun-Ho. Sorry I'**m** late for our meeting.
Mr. Garcia	That'**s** OK. Nice to meet you, Jun-Ho. Please have a seat.
5 *Jun-Ho*	Thanks.
Mr. Garcia	First, I'**m** glad that you'**re** here. As your adviser, I'**m** here to help you. I can help you choose your classes, and I can help you with any problems.
10 *Jun-Ho*	Thanks, I need your help. I have lots of questions about courses, instructors, and my program.
Mr. Garcia	Good! But first I'd like to know more about you. Tell me about yourself.
Jun-Ho	Sure. I'**m** 19, and I'**m** a graduate of Central High School. I'**m** from 15 South Korea originally.
Mr. Garcia	I see. What **are** some of your interests?
Jun-Ho	Well, I'**m** interested in cars and music. And I really like computers. My major **is** computer science.
Mr. Garcia	Great. You know, the college has lots of clubs. It'**s** a good way to 20 meet people and practice English.
Jun-Ho	Well, I'**m** pretty busy most of the time. My brother and I **are** salesclerks in my uncle's store. We'**re** really interested in his business. I don't have much free time.
Mr. Garcia	OK. I understand. Now, let's talk about your academic plans . . .

2

B *Comprehension Check* Circle the correct words.

1. Mr. Garcia is **a student / an adviser**.

2. Jun-Ho is from **South Korea / the United States**.

3. Jun-Ho is a salesclerk in his uncle's **store / restaurant**.

C *Notice* Complete the sentences. Use the conversation to help you.

1. I _____ Jun-Ho. Sorry I _____ late.

2. My major _____ computer science.

3. My brother and I _____ salesclerks. We _____ really interested in his business.

2 | Present of *Be*: Affirmative Statements

▶ Grammar Presentation

Be links ideas.	I 'm a student.

2.1 Full Forms (with Subject Pronouns)

SINGULAR		
Subject	***Be***	
I	**am**	late.
You	**are**	
He She It	**is**	
		difficult.

PLURAL		
Subject	***Be***	
We You They	**are**	from Seoul.

▸◂ Capitalization and Punctuation Rules: See page A1.

2.2 Contractions (with Nouns and Subject Pronouns)

SINGULAR			PLURAL		
I am	→	I'**m**	We are	→	We'**re**
You are	→	You'**re**	You are	→	You'**re**
He is	→	He'**s**	They are	→	They'**re**
Jun-Ho is	→	Jun-Ho'**s**			
She is	→	She'**s**			
His mother is	→	His mother'**s**			
It is	→	It'**s**			
My name is	→	My name'**s**			

2.3 Using Present of *Be*

a. The verb *be* "links" ideas. You can use *be* to link nouns or pronouns with words that give information about them.	Jun-Ho is a student. They are from California.
b. Use the full forms of *be* in academic writing.	I **am** a computer science major. I **am** in your grammar class.
c. Use contractions of *be* in conversation and informal writing.	I'**m** Mr. Garcia. They'**re** sick today.
d. You can use *be* + noun • to talk about occupations.	He's **a teacher**. They're **students**.
• to identify things.	It's an **English class**. My hobbies are **baseball and music**. My major is **math**.
e. You can use *be* + number to talk about ages.	My sister is **18**. His parents are **49** years old.
f. You can use *be* + adjective • to talk about nationalities.	I'm **Canadian**. His parents are **South Korean**.
• to describe people and things.	Jun-Ho is **tall**. My sister is **sick**. Our reading class is **interesting**.

2.3 Using Present of *Be* *(continued)*

g. You can use *be* + preposition	
• to talk about hometowns and places.	*My parents are **from Seoul**.* *I'm **from California**.*
• to talk about where people and things are.	*She is **at home**.* *We are **in Los Angeles**.*
• to talk about the groups, such as teams or clubs, that people are in.	*My friends and I are **in a band**.* *He is **on the basketball team**.*

▶ Grammar Application

Exercise 2.1 Present of *Be*: Full Forms

A Complete the sentences about a student, using *am*, *is*, and *are*.

1. My name is Ling. I _am_ a student at the University of Florida.

2. My friend Ana and I _____ in Science 101.

3. Mr. Johnson _____ a good instructor.

4. The class _____ interesting.

5. My classmates _____ crazy about science.

6. Ana _____ smart.

7. Ana and I _____ seniors this year.

B Look at the underlined word(s). Circle the subject pronoun that replaces the underlined words.

1. My college is in Detroit, Michigan. **It / She** is a good school.

2. Jorge and Lisa are in Grammar 110. **They / We** are in a fun class.

3. Mrs. Chapple is a great teacher. **It / She** is also very nice.

4. Marcos is crazy about grammar. **He / They** is never late for class.

5. My brother is smart. **He / It** is an excellent student.

6. My mother is a nurse. **She / It** is always very busy.

7. My sister and I are sick. **She / We** are at home today.

C Complete the student's online profile. Use the full forms of *be* (*am, is, are*).

My name __is__ Cindy Wang. I _____ from
(1)   (2)
Jackson, Illinois. My parents _____ from China
(3)
originally. I _____ 20 years old. I _____ now
(4)   (5)
a student at the University of Texas. My major _____
(6)
public health. My favorite subjects _____ math and
(7)
biology. I _____ interested in sports and drawing.
(8)
My friend Bev and I _____ servers in a restaurant on
(9)
weekends. My sister _____ still a high school student in Illinois.
(10)

D *Over to You* Complete the sentences with the correct full form of *be* and the information about you. Then read your sentences to your partner. How many of your sentences are the same?

1. My name _____ _____ .
            (be)   (name)

2. I _____ from _____ .
      (be)   (country)

3. I _____ _____ .
      (be)   (age)

4. My major _____ _____ .
            (be)   (subject)

5. My favorite class _____ _____ .
                    (be)   (name of class)

6. I _____ interested in _____ .
      (be)   (name of things)

7. I _____ .
   (Tell one more thing about yourself. Remember to use *be*.)

Exercise 2.2 Present of *Be*: Contractions

A Complete the sentences with *'m, 's,* or *'re.*

1. *Ana* Hi, I __'m__ Ana.
              (1)

    Ron Hi, Ana. My name_____ Ron. Nice to meet you.
                            (2)

    Ana It_____ nice to meet you, too.
              (3)

    Ron I_____ in Ms. Cook's class.
             (4)

    Ana She_____ my teacher, too. You_____ in
                (5)   (6)
           my class.

    Ron Great. I think we_____ in Room 9.
                              (7)

2. *Sara* Excuse me. I'm lost. My teacher_____ Mr. Martinez.
         (8)

   Ron Mr. Martinez? He_____ in Room 10.
         (9)

   Ana Room 10_____ over there. On the right.
         (10)

   Sara Oh, thanks.

   Ana You_____ welcome.
         (11)

3. *Ana* Ron, this is my friend Cathy. We_____ friends from
         (12)

   high school.

   Ron Hi, Cathy.

   Cathy Hi, Ron!

   Ana Cathy_____ on the basketball team. She_____ a
         (13)   (14)

   great player.

   Ron Really? I_____ a big basketball fan.
         (15)

   Ana Well, come to our next game. It_____ on Friday.
         (16)

B *Pair Work* Introduce yourself to your partner. Use contractions. Then introduce your
partner to a classmate.

Hi, I'm Alex. This is Hong-yin. He's from Texas. He's on the soccer team.

3 | Present of *Be*: Negative Statements

▶ Grammar Presentation

3.1 Full Forms

SINGULAR				PLURAL		
Subject	***Be + Not***			**Subject**	***Be + Not***	
I	**am not**			We		
You	**are not**		in class.	You	**are not**	students.
He She It	**is not**			They		

3.2 Negative Contractions

SINGULAR			PLURAL		
I am not	→	I**'m not**	We are not	→	We**'re not** / We **aren't**
You are not	→	You**'re not** / You **aren't**	You are not	→	You**'re not** / You **aren't**
He is not	→	He**'s not** / He **isn't**	They are not	→	They**'re not** / They **aren't**
She is not	→	She**'s not** / She **isn't**			
It is not	→	It**'s not** / It **isn't**			

Data from the Real World

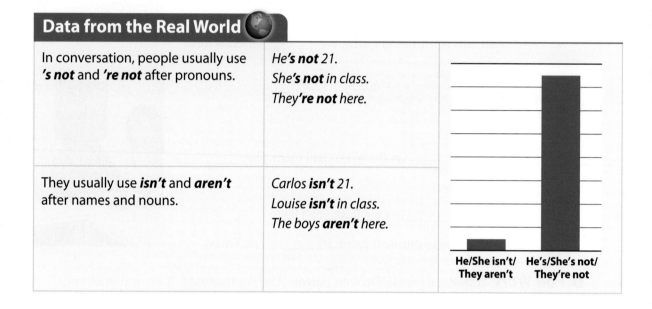

In conversation, people usually use **'s not** and **'re not** after pronouns.	He**'s not** 21. She**'s not** in class. They**'re not** here.
They usually use **isn't** and **aren't** after names and nouns.	Carlos **isn't** 21. Louise **isn't** in class. The boys **aren't** here.

He/She isn't/   He's/She's not/
They aren't   They're not

▶ Grammar Application

Exercise 3.1 Present of *Be:* Negative Statements with Full Forms

A Complete the sentences. Use *am not*, *is not*, or *are not*.

1. My roommate and I _*are not*_ math majors.

2. My friends _____ in my business class.

3. My cousin _____ married.

4. You _____ late.

5. My friend _____ in the library.

6. I _____ interested in chemistry.

7. Our instructor _____ from the United States.

8. The students _____ interested in history.

B *Over to You* Write six negative sentences about yourself. Use the full form of *be*.

1. I _am not_ a teacher.
2. I _____ from _____ .
3. I _____ interested in _____ .
4. I _____ a/an _____ major.
5. I _____ a/an _____ .
6. I _____ in _____ .

C *Pair Work* Read your sentences to a partner. Are any of your sentences the same?

Exercise 3.2 Affirmative or Negative?

A Read the online profiles. Complete the sentences with the correct affirmative or negative form of *be*. Use contractions when possible.

	Yoko Akeda	Luiz da Costa
Age	21	35
Hometown	Los Angeles, California	New York, New York
Occupation or job; location	student at Glen College	instructor at Glen College
Interested in . . .	music, art museums	music, biking
Not interested in . . .	cooking, computer games	movies, cooking
Favorite TV show	*The Race*	*American Idol*

1. Yoko _is_ 21. She _'s not_ 35.
2. Yoko and Luiz _____ the same age.
3. Luiz _____ an instructor. He _____ a student.
4. Yoko _____ from New York. She _____ from Los Angeles.
5. Luiz _____ from New York. He _____ from Los Angeles.
6. They _____ from Chicago.
7. They _____ interested in music.
   They _____ interested in cooking.
8. Luiz _____ interested in movies.
9. *American Idol* _____ Yoko's favorite TV show.
10. *The Race* _____ Yoko's favorite TV show. It _____ Luiz's favorite show.

B ◄)) Listen. Where are these people? Complete the sentences with the correct pronouns and forms of *be*. Use contractions when possible.

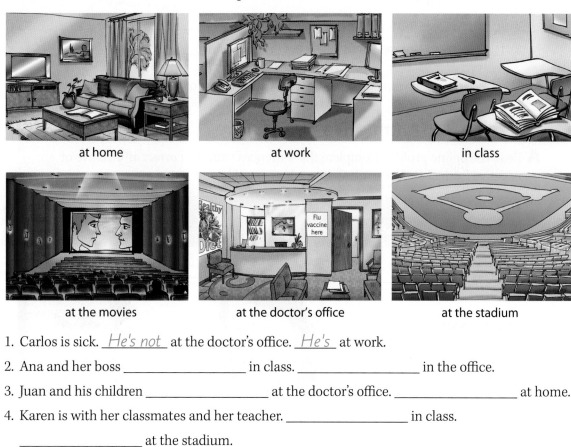

at home   at work   in class

at the movies   at the doctor's office   at the stadium

1. Carlos is sick. _He's not_ at the doctor's office. _He's_ at work.

2. Ana and her boss _____ in class. _____ in the office.

3. Juan and his children _____ at the doctor's office. _____ at home.

4. Karen is with her classmates and her teacher. _____ in class.
   _____ at the stadium.

5. David is a big baseball fan. _____ at the stadium. _____ at home.

6. Ling and John are interested in movies. _____ at Drew's apartment.
   _____ at the movies.

C *Pair Work* Tell a partner about four people you know. Where are they today?

My brother is at work. He's a salesclerk in a store . . .

Exercise 3.3 Negative of *Be*

Complete the conversations. Use *'s not* and *'re not* after pronouns and *isn't* and *aren't* after names and nouns.

1. **Sara** Hello. Accounting Department.

   Ben Louise?

   Sara No, it's Sara. Louise _isn't_ here.
   (1)
   She _____ at work today.
   (2)

2. *Sam*   Oh, no! My wallet _____ in my bag!
                        (3)
           It's on the bus!

  Man   No, it _____ on the bus.
                    (4)
           Look, here it is.

3. *Lara*   Where are your brothers? The game's on TV,

        and they _____ here.
                (5)
   Joe   They _____ interested in baseball.
              (6)
      They _____ interested in sports.
            (7)

4 Avoid Common Mistakes ⚠️

1. Use *be* to link ideas.

    is
He ⌄an engineering student.

2. Use *be* + *not* to form negative statements with *be*. Do not use *be* + *no*.

    not
Ana is ~~no~~ a science teacher.

3. A statement has a subject. Do not begin a statement with *be*.

She is
~~Is~~ my sister's best friend.

Editing Task

Correct nine more mistakes about Amy. Rewrite the sentences.

1. This my friend. *This is my friend.* _____

2. Her name Amy. _____

3. Amy and I roommates. _____

4. She 27. _____

5. She is no a student. _____

6. Is a science teacher. _____

7. Is very nice and very smart. _____

8. Amy is no in school today. _____

9. She sick. _____

10. Is at home. _____

5 Grammar for Writing

Writing About a Person

Writers often use the verb *be* when they describe people. Remember:

- ***Be* + noun can tell an occupation or identify people.**
  Marisol is my friend. She is a graduate student.

- ***Be* + number can tell a person's age.**
  Marisol is not old. She is only 28 years old.

- ***Be* + adjective tells a person's nationality or describes a person.**
  Marisol is Peruvian. She is very friendly.

- ***Be* + preposition can give a location or tell a group that a person belongs to.**
  Marisol is from California. She is in Paris right now. She is on a soccer team.

Pre-writing Task

1 Read the paragraph below. Who is the important person?

An Important Person in My Life

My sister is an important person in my life. Her name is Lila. She is 23 years old. She is a nurse at Cottage Hospital. Her interests are dancing and music. She is not interested in sports. She is tall. Her hair is long, and she is very beautiful. She is also very funny. She is still single. She and I are good friends. We are together often.

2 Read the paragraph again. Circle every form of the verb *be*. How many times does the verb *be* appear in the paragraph?

Writing Task

1 *Write* Use the paragraph in the Pre-writing Task to help you write about an important person in your life. Write at least four things about this person. For example, tell about the person's age, occupation, nationality, appearance, personality, or interests.

2 *Self-Edit* Use the editing tips below to improve your sentences. Make any necessary changes.

1. Did you use the verb *be* to tell many things about the important person in your life?
2. Did you use the correct form of *be* in your sentences?
3. Did your sentences all have a subject?
4. Did you avoid the mistakes in the Avoid Common Mistakes chart on page 11?

Yes / No Questions and Information Questions with *Be*

Schedules and School

1 Grammar in the Real World

A 🔊 What is your class schedule? Read and listen to the conversations below. Are Yuko's and Juan's classes the same?

Conversation A (Monday)

Yuko So, **is your next class writing?**

Juan No, it's reading.

Yuko Really? My next class is reading, too. **Are you in my class?** It's at 1:30.

Juan Maybe. **Is your class in Building H?**

Yuko Yes, it's in Building H, Room 308.

10 *Juan* Then I'm in your class, too!

Yuko Hmm. **Where's Building H?**

Juan It's on the hill, over there.

Yuko Oh, OK. **What time is it?**

Juan It's 1:20. Uh-oh. We're late!

15 *Yuko* No, we aren't.

Juan **Are you sure?**

Yuko Yes. Class is at 1:30.

Juan Oh, you're right. That's good. Let's go.

Conversation B (Thursday)

Yuko Hey, Juan. **How are you?** 20

Juan I'm OK. **How are you?**

Yuko I'm fine, thanks.

Juan **How are your classes?**

Yuko They're fine, but they're all really big. 25

Juan Really? **How many students are in your classes?**

Yuko About 25 to 30. **Is that unusual?**

Juan No, it isn't. **Who's your** 30 **grammar teacher?**

Yuko Mr. Walters. He's funny, but his class is difficult.

Juan So, **when's your next class?**

Yuko Let me see. Today's Thursday. 35 Computer lab is at 3:00.

Juan **When is it over?**

Yuko At 4:15. Let's meet after that.

B *Comprehension Check* Read the sentences. Circle *True* or *False*.

Conversation A

1. Yuko and Juan are in Building H now.   True   False

2. They are late for class.   True   False

Conversation B

3. Mr. Walters is Yuko's grammar teacher.   True   False

4. Computer lab is over at 4:15.   True   False

C *Notice* Find the questions in the conversations. Complete the questions.

1. _____ you in my class?

2. _____ your class in Building H?

3. _____ that unusual?

4. _____ you sure?

Which words are at the beginning of the questions?

2 | Yes / No Questions and Short Answers with *Be*

▶ Grammar Presentation

A *Yes / No* question is a question you can answer with *Yes* or *No*.	"Is Yuko's class in Building H?" "Yes, it is." / "No, it isn't."

2.1 Singular *Yes / No* Questions

Be	Subject	
Am	I	
Are	you	in class?
Is	he / she / it	

2.2 Singular Short Answers

AFFIRMATIVE				NEGATIVE		
	Subject	*Be*			Subject	*Be + Not*
	I	**am.**			I	**am not.**
Yes,	you	**are.**		No,	you	**are not.**
	he / she / it	**is.**			he / she / it	**is not.**

2.3 Plural *Yes* / *No* Questions

Be	Subject	
Are	we you they	late?

2.4 Plural Short Answers

AFFIRMATIVE				NEGATIVE			
	Subject	*Be*			Subject	*Be + Not*	
Yes,	we you they	**are**.		No,	we you they	**are not**.	

2.5 Negative Short Answers: Contractions

SINGULAR			PLURAL	
No, I am not.	→	No, I**'m not**.	No, we are not. →	No, we**'re not**. No, we **aren't**.
No, you are not.	→	No, you**'re not**. No, you **aren't**.	No, you are not. →	No, you**'re not**. No, you **aren't**.
No, he is not.	→	No, he**'s not**. No, he **isn't**.	No, they are not. →	No, they**'re not**. No, they **aren't**.
No, she is not.	→	No, she**'s not**. No, she **isn't**.		
No, it is not.	→	No, it**'s not**. No, it **isn't**.		

3.4 Using *Wh-* Words with *Be* (continued)

d. Use *when* to ask about days or times.	**When's** your exam? **When** is lunch? **When** are our exams?	It's February 14. At noon. Next week.
e. Use *how* to ask about health or opinions.	**How's** your mother? **How's** school?	She's well. Great!
f. Use *how much* to ask about cost and amount. Use *how many* to ask about numbers. Use *how old* to ask about age.	**How much** is the movie? **How many** students are here? **How old** are your brothers?	Eight dollars. Twelve. They're 17 and 15.

▶ Grammar Application

Exercise 3.1 Information Questions with *Be*

A Complete the conversation between Joe and his mother. Use the correct *Wh-* word. Use contractions of *be*.

Mother   <u>*What's*</u> your roommate's name?
          (1)
    Joe   Mike.

Mother   _____ he from?
              (2)
    Joe   Chicago.

Mother   _____ his major?
              (3)
    Joe   I don't know. Mom, my history class is in five minutes.

Mother   _____ your instructor?
              (4)
    Joe   I don't know his name. It's the first class.

Mother   _____ your class over?
              (5)
    Joe   At 4:30. Please don't call before that.

B Complete the questions with *How*, *How much*, *How many*, or *How old*. Use the correct form of *be*.

1. <u>*How are*</u> you?   I'm fine, thanks.
2. _____ you?   I'm 23.
3. _____ the textbook?   It's $26.
4. _____ students _____ in your English class?   Thirty.
5. _____ the sandwiches?   They're $5.75.

Exercise 3.2 Information Questions and Answers

Write questions about the tuition bill. Then write answers in complete sentences.

Plains Community College

Spring Semester   February 1–May 28
Name: Jason Armenio   **Student ID Number:** 452319
Major: History   **Total class credits:** 15

    Tuition: $ 600.00   ($40.00 per credit)
    Parking permit: $ 20.00
    Health Services Fee: $ 17.00
  Total: **$ 637.00**

IMPORTANT DATES
First day of classes: February 1 **Tuition payment due:** January 31
Spring Break: March 29–April 3 **Final Exams:** May 24–28

1. (What / the college's name) *What is the college's name? It's Plains Community College.*

2. (What / the student's name) _____

3. (When / the spring semester) _____

4. (What / his major) _____

5. (How much / the tuition) _____

6. (How much / the parking permit) _____

7. (What / the total) _____

8. (When / final exams) _____

Exercise 3.3 More Information Questions and Answers

Pair Work With a partner, write five questions to ask your classmates. Ask questions about their classes, schedules, and school. Then interview your classmates. Write their answers in the chart.

Interview Questions	Your Classmates' Answers
1. *When are your classes?*	*My classes are on Monday and Wednesday.*
2.	
3.	
4.	
5.	
6.	

4 Avoid Common Mistakes ⚠️

1. Begin a question with a capital letter. End with a question mark.

$\overset{W}{\cancel{w}}$here is Karla$\overset{?}{\cancel{/}}$

2. Remember that a question has a subject and a verb.

Where $\overset{is}{\wedge}$ Room 203?

3. Don't use contractions with short *Yes* answers to *Yes / No* questions.

"Are you tired?"   "Yes, $\overset{I\ am}{\cancel{I'm}}$."

4. Make sure the subject and verb agree.

$\overset{Are}{\cancel{Is}}$ John and Pedro here?

5. Put the verb after the question word in information questions.

When is the writing class?
~~When the writing class is?~~

Editing Task

Find and correct the mistakes in these questions and answers about your school.

1. $\overset{W}{\cancel{w}}$here is your school?

2. What is the school's name.

3. How much the tuition is?

4. "your school expensive."   "Yes, it's."

5. What your major?

6. Is you a good student?

7. When summer break is?

8. Is all your classes difficult?

5 | Grammar for Writing ✎

Using Questions to Get Information About a Topic

Writers use questions to get information about topics they want to write about. First, they think of the information that they want to know. Then they ask the questions that will give them that information.

Remember:

Question word order and statement word order are different.

	SUBJECT	VERB	
Statement	*Paulo*	*is*	*at the library.*
	VERB	SUBJECT	
Yes/No Question	*Is*	*Paulo*	*at the library?*
	WH- WORD	VERB	SUBJECT
Information Question	*Where*	*is*	*Paulo?*

Pre-writing Task

1 Read the paragraph below.

My Classmate Javier

Javier is a college student. His school is in Orlando, Florida. His major is business. His business classes are all interesting. His first language is Spanish. His birthday is on June 11. His interests are computers and soccer. He is married, and his wife's name is Violeta. She is not a student.

2 Write the questions the writer asked Javier to get information before writing the paragraph.

Writer's Questions	Javier's Answers
1. Are __*you a student*__ ?	Yes, I am.
2. Where _____ ?	It's in Orlando, Florida.
3. What _____ ?	It's business.
4. How _____ ?	They're all interesting.
5. What _____ ?	It's Spanish.
6. When _____ ?	It's on June 11.
7. What _____ ?	Computers and soccer.

8. _____ married?   Yes, I am.

9. What _____ ?   Violeta.

10. _____ a student?   No, she isn't.

Writing Task

1 *Write*   Use the paragraph in the Pre-writing Task to help you write about a classmate or a friend. Decide on the information you want to know. Then write at least six questions to find out the answers. Interview the person, and then write your paragraph.

2 *Self-Edit*   Use the editing tips below to improve your sentences. Make any necessary changes.

1. Did you use questions to find out information about your classmate?
2. Did you use the correct word order for *Yes / No* questions?
3. Did you use the correct word order for information questions?
4. Did you avoid the mistakes in the Avoid Common Mistakes chart on page 23?

Count Nouns; *A/An*; *Have* and *Be*

Gadgets

1 Grammar in the Real World

A Do you have a cell phone? If so, is your cell phone like these phones? Read the web page. Which phone is best for you?

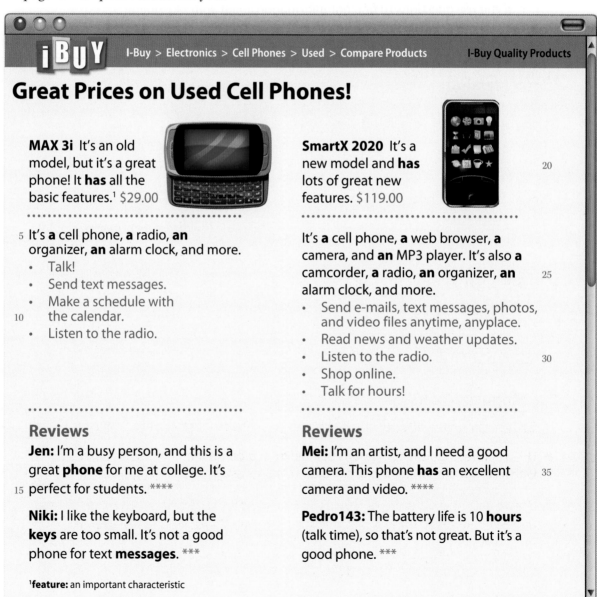

i**BUY**   I-Buy > Electronics > Cell Phones > Used > Compare Products   **I-Buy Quality Products**

Great Prices on Used Cell Phones!

MAX 3i It's an old model, but it's a great phone! It **has** all the basic features.[1] $29.00

5 It's **a** cell phone, **a** radio, **an** organizer, **an** alarm clock, and more.
- Talk!
- Send text messages.
- Make a schedule with
10   the calendar.
- Listen to the radio.

SmartX 2020 It's a new model and **has** lots of great new features. $119.00   20

It's **a** cell phone, **a** web browser, **a** camera, and **an** MP3 player. It's also **a** camcorder, **a** radio, **an** organizer, **an**   25 alarm clock, and more.
- Send e-mails, text messages, photos, and video files anytime, anyplace.
- Read news and weather updates.
- Listen to the radio.   30
- Shop online.
- Talk for hours!

Reviews

Jen: I'm a busy person, and this is a great **phone** for me at college. It's
15 perfect for students. ****

Niki: I like the keyboard, but the **keys** are too small. It's not a good phone for text **messages**. ***

Reviews

Mei: I'm an artist, and I need a good camera. This phone **has** an excellent   35 camera and video. ****

Pedro143: The battery life is 10 **hours** (talk time), so that's not great. But it's a good phone. ***

[1]**feature:** an important characteristic

B *Comprehension Check* Answer the questions. Circle *Yes* or *No*. Use the web page to help you.

1. Are the two phones new models?   Yes   No

2. Is the MAX 3i $29.00?   Yes   No

3. Is the SmartX 2020's camera good?   Yes   No

C *Notice* Circle the correct words. Use the web page to help you.

1. The MAX 3i is **a / an** old model.

2. Jen is **a / an** busy person.

3. The battery life is 10 **hour / hours**.

4. This is a great **phone / phones** for me.

2 | Nouns; *A/An*

▶ Grammar Presentation

Nouns are words for people, places, and things.	*I'm an* **artist**. *It's an electronics* **store**. *It is a great* **phone**. *They are great* **phones**.

2.1 Singular and Plural Nouns

Singular Nouns	Plural Nouns
It's a **camera**.	*They are* **cameras**.
It's a good **product**.	*They are good* **products**.

2.2 Singular Nouns

a. Count nouns have singular and plural forms.	*a book – three books* *one phone – two phones*
b. Use *a* before singular count nouns that begin with a consonant sound (*b, c, d, f, g*, etc.).	*a* **cell** *phone* *a* **web** *browser* *a* **screen** *a camera*
c. Use *an* before singular count nouns that begin with a vowel sound (*a, e, i, o, u*).	*an* **address** *book* *an* **advertisement** *an* **MP3** *player* *an* **update**
Note: Some nouns that begin with the letter *u* have a consonant sound ("you").	*a* **unit** *a university*

▸▸ Indefinite and Definite Articles: See page A19.

2.3 Plural Nouns

a. Add *-s* to most singular nouns to form plural nouns.	*a model – two model***s** *a key – key***s**	*a camera – two camera***s** *a student – student***s**
b. Add *-es* to nouns that end in *-ch*, *-sh*, *-ss*, *-z*, and *-x*.	*watch – watch***es** *dish – dish***es**	*class – class***es** *tax – tax***es**
c. With nouns that end in consonant + *y*, change the *y* to *i* and add *-es*.	*battery – batter***ies**	*accessory – accessor***ies**
d. With nouns that end in *-ife*, change the ending to *-ives*.	*life – l***ives**	*knife – kn***ives**

2.4 Irregular Plural Nouns

a. Some plural nouns have irregular forms.	*man – men* *child – children* *foot – feet*	*woman – women* *person – people* *tooth – teeth*
These are the most common irregular plural nouns in academic writing.		
b. Some nouns have the same form for singular and plural.	*one fish – two fish*	*one sheep – two sheep*
c. Some nouns are only plural. They do not have a singular form.	*clothes* *jeans* *headphones* *pants*	*scissors* *sunglasses*

▶▶ Spelling Rules for Noun Plurals: See page A2.

2.5 Proper Nouns

Proper nouns are the names of specific people, places, and things. They begin with capital letters.	*Jenny* *Mr. Johns* *Canada* *Dallas* *San Francisco Herald*	*Ms. Thorson* *Chester College*

▶▶ Capitalization and Punctuation Rules: See page A1.

▶ Grammar Application

Exercise 2.1 *A* or *An*

A Write *a* or *an* next to each noun.

1. _*a*_ pencil
2. _____ eraser
3. _____ camera
4. _____ grammar book
5. _____ laptop
6. _____ marker
7. _____ address book
8. _____ calculator
9. _____ wallet
10. _____ notebook

B *Over to You* Ask and answer questions about things in the classroom. Use *a* or *an*. Make a list of the new words you learn.

> A *What's the word for this in English?*
> B *It's a desk. / I don't know. Let's ask the teacher.*

Exercise 2.2 Plural Nouns

A Look at this store advertisement. Write the plural form of the nouns. For nouns that have only one form, leave the space blank.

Shop at **The Mart**

This week's sale prices

Electronics		School Supply*ies*		Clothes and Accessory____	
battery_____	$3–$5	dictionary_____	$5.95–$29.95	dress_____	$19–$89
calculator_____	$8–$75	scissors_____	$2.95–$10	belt_____	$13–$39
headphones_____	$5–$65	notebook_____	75¢–$3.50	sunglasses_____	$10–$20
cell phone_____	$60–$200			purse_____	$19–$129
computer_____	$300–$999			jeans_____	$29–$80
video camera_____	$400–$1,000				

B *Pair Work* Practice asking and answering questions about the items in A with a partner.

> A *How much are the belts?*
> B *They're $13 to $39.*

Exercise 2.3 ◀)) Pronunciation Focus: Plural Nouns

For nouns that end in the sounds /s/, /ʃ/, /tʃ/, /dʒ/, /ks/, and /z/, say /əz/ in the plural. These nouns have an extra syllable in the plural form.		**/əz/**
	/s/	class – classes
	/ʃ/	di**sh** – di**sh**es
	/tʃ/	wat**ch** – wat**ch**es
	/dʒ/	messa**ge** – messa**ge**s
	/ks/	bo**x** – bo**x**es
	/z/	qui**z** – qui**zz**es
For most other nouns, say /s/ or /z/ in the plural.		**/s/ or /z/**
		boo**k** – boo**k**s
		ph**one** – ph**one**s
		accessor**y** – accessor**ies**

A 🔊)) Listen. Check (✓) the nouns with an extra syllable in the plural form.

☑ 1. purse – purses   ☐ 4. door – doors   ☐ 7. page – pages

☐ 2. bag – bags   ☐ 5. size – sizes   ☐ 8. closet – closets

☐ 3. map – maps   ☐ 6. computer – computers   ☐ 9. phone – phones

B Write the plural form of these nouns. Do they have an extra syllable? Check (✓) *Yes* or *No*.

	Extra Syllable?				Extra Syllable?	
	Yes	**No**			**Yes**	**No**
1. desk _desks_	☐	☑	8. brush _____		☐	☐
2. tax _____	☐	☐	9. dictionary _____		☐	☐
3. CD player _____	☐	☐	10. match _____		☐	☐
4. case _____	☐	☐	11. chair _____		☐	☐
5. orange _____	☐	☐	12. quiz _____		☐	☐
6. penny _____	☐	☐	13. pen _____		☐	☐
7. student _____	☐	☐	14. garage _____		☐	☐

Exercise 2.4 Proper Nouns

Write answers to the questions. Use proper nouns.

1. What's the capital of the United States? _It's Washington, D.C._____

2. What's your last name? _____

3. What's the name of the street where you live? _____

4. What's the name of your hometown? _____

5. What's the name of your favorite movie? _____

6. What's your favorite store? _____

7. What's the name of your school or college? _____

8. What's your teacher's name? _____

3 | *Be* with *A/An* + Noun

▶ Grammar Presentation

3.1 Using *Be* with *A/An* + Noun

a. You can use *be* with *a/an* + noun to tell: • what something is. • what something is like. • who someone is. • what someone is like.	*It's **a** cell phone. It's **an** MP3 player, too.* *It's **a** great phone.* *Jon is **a** friend from college.* *He's **a** nice guy.*
b. You can use *be* + *a/an* + noun to say a person's occupation.	*Jenny is **a** businesswoman.* *Pedro is **an** architect.*
c. Don't use *a/an* with plural nouns.	*They're cell phone**s**.* NOT *They are a cell phones.*

Pronunciation note: *A* and *an* are not usually stressed. *a* = /ə/ and *an* = /ən/
/ə/ CELL phone   /ən/ ARchitect

▶ Grammar Application

Exercise 3.1 *A/An* + Noun

Complete the conversation with *a* or *an*.

A Is that ___*a*___ new cell phone? Is it _____ MP3 player, too?
　　　　　　(1)　　　　　　　　　　　　(2)

B Yes. It's my new toy. It's _____ smart phone.
　　　　　　　　　　　　　　(3)

A Cool. Oh, look! Is that _____ e-mail?
　　　　　　　　　　　　(4)

B No, it's _____ text message from Jeff.
　　　　　　(5)

A Jeff? Is he _____ friend?
　　　　　　　(6)

B Yes, from high school. He's now _____ engineering
　　　　　　　　　　　　　　　　　(7)

student at _____ university in Florida. He's in town
　　　　　(8)

with his brother, Dan. Dan's _____ artist.
　　　　　　　　　　　　　(9)

A Wow. So, where are they?

B They're at _____ coffee shop near here. Let's go see them.
　　　　　(10)

A That sounds like fun. Let's get _____ taxi.
　　　　　　　　　　　　　　(11)

Exercise 3.2 *A / An* + Noun: Occupations

A Match the occupations and the pictures. Write the correct letter next to the names.
Then complete the sentences below. Make some occupations plural.

| a. chef | b. electrician | ¢. engineer | d. mechanic | e. pharmacist | f. receptionist |

1. Mike __*c*__

2. Carl _____

3. Julia _____

4. Jody and Bryan _____

5. Sarah _____

6. Ana and Peter _____

1. Mike *is an engineer.* _____

2. Carl _____

3. Julia _____

4. Jody and Bryan _____

5. Sarah _____

6. Ana and Peter _____

B *Over to You* Write sentences about people you know.

1. I am <u>*a student. I'm also a part-time salesclerk.*</u>

2. My friend is _____

3. My neighbor is _____

4. My friends are _____ and _____ . They _____

5. My classmate's name is _____ . He / She _____

6. My _____ is _____
   (family member)

4 | *Have*

▶ Grammar Presentation

Have can show possession. It can also mean "to experience."	He **has** a nice apartment. (possession) My friends and I **have** a good time together. (experience)

4.1 *Have*

Subject	*Have*	
I We You They	**have**	a camera.
He She It	**has**	

4.2 Using *Have*

a. Use *have* + noun to show:

- possession or ownership.
- relationships.
- parts of a whole.

I **have** a car.
She **has** a friend from Chile.
The website **has** helpful links.

b. It can also mean "to experience" or "to take part in an activity."

We **have** fun in class.
They **have** lunch at 12:30.

▶ Grammar Application

Exercise 4.1 *Have*

Complete the sentences. Use *have* or *has*.

1. Big Electric is an electronics store. It usually __*has*__ good prices.

2. The store is very large. It _____ four floors.

3. The first floor _____ computers and phones.

4. The second floor _____ video game consoles and video games.

5. The third and fourth floors _____ TVs, sound systems, and entertainment systems.

6. Big Electric also _____ a website.

7. The website sometimes _____ special sale prices.

8. Customers _____ a lot of fun shopping here.

Exercise 4.2 *Have* and *Be*

Complete the sentences from a student essay. Use *have, has, am, is,* or *are.*

My Favorite Gadget

Let me tell you about my laptop. It __*is*__ an old laptop, but it _____ a good
                                   (1)   (2)
computer. It only weighs four pounds, so it _____ not very heavy. It _____
                                            (3)   (4)
great speakers, and it also _____ a bright, colorful screen. So it _____ great for
                            (5)   (6)
movies and for music. It _____ also good for e-mail. I _____ a student, so my
                         (7)   (8)
laptop _____ very important for me. I use it to do almost all my homework. This
       (9)
laptop also _____ a webcam. I use it to talk to my friends in Mexico. I _____ a lot
            (10)   (11)
of friends there, and we _____ very happy to see each other and talk over
                         (12)
the Internet. Sometimes I _____ problems with my computer. For example, the
                          (13)
battery _____ not very strong. Also, the computer _____ slow. I want a new
        (14)   (15)
one, but good laptops _____ very expensive.
                      (16)

Writing Task

1 *Write* Use the paragraph in the Pre-writing Task to help you write about a favorite city or place. Write about the places and things that make this place special.

2 *Self-Edit* Use the editing tips below to improve your sentences. Make any necessary changes.

1. Did you use sentences with *be* and *have* to tell about your favorite place?
2. Did you use *be* to describe people and things?
3. Did you use *have* to show possession and experience?
4. Did you avoid the mistakes in the Avoid Common Mistakes chart on page 35?

1 | Grammar in the Real World

A Can you name five things that you use in an office? Read the conversation. How many different office things do the speakers mention in the conversation?

First Day at the Office

Robert	Hello, Claudia. I'm Robert. Welcome to **our** company!
Claudia	Hello, Robert. It's nice to meet you.
Robert	**This** is **your** desk. **That**'s the closet for **your** coat. Let me show you around.
5 *Claudia*	Thanks.
Robert	Office supplies, like paper, folders, and CDs, are in **those** cabinets over there. The printers are here, and **this** is the only copy machine. The paper is in **these** drawers below the printers.

Claudia	Thanks. **That**'s good to know.
10 *Robert*	Now, let me introduce you to Keung. He's on **your** team. Keung, **this** is Claudia. She's **our** new sales manager.
Keung	Nice to meet you, Claudia.
Claudia	Nice to meet you, Keung. **Those** photographs are beautiful. Are you a photographer?
15 *Keung*	Well, photography is **my** hobby. **Those** pictures are from **my** trip to Thailand.
Claudia	**That** photograph on the left is great. What is it?
Keung	It's the Royal Palace in Bangkok, **my** favorite place.
Claudia	**That**'s a great picture, too.
20 *Keung*	**Those** little girls are **my sister's** children. She lives in Bangkok.
Robert	Sorry to interrupt, but we have a management meeting in 10 minutes. It's in the conference room. It's **this** way, down the hall. Let's get some coffee before the meeting.
Claudia	OK. See you later, Keung.
25 *Keung*	Wait. Robert, are **these your** reports?
Robert	Yes, they are. Thanks. I need them for the meeting.

B *Comprehension Check* Match the two parts of the sentences about the conversation.

1. Claudia _____   a. are in the cabinets.

2. Keung _____   b. are his sister's children.

3. The little girls in the photograph _____   c. is a new employee.

4. Office supplies _____   d. is in the conference room.

5. The meeting _____   e. is on her team.

C *Notice* Find the sentences in the conversation and circle the correct words.

1. The paper is in **these** / **this** *drawers* below the printers.

2. **Those** / **That** *photograph* on the left is great.

3. **That** / **Those** little *girls* are my sister's children.

4. It's **this** / **these** *way*, down the hall.

Now look at the nouns in *italics*. What words come before the singular nouns? What words come before the plural nouns?

2 Demonstratives (*This, That, These, Those*)

▶ Grammar Presentation

The demonstratives are *this, that, these*, and *those*. We use demonstratives to "point to" things and people.	**This** is my desk. **Those** desks are for new employees.

2.1 Demonstratives with Singular and Plural Nouns

SINGULAR				PLURAL			
This / That	Noun	Verb		*These / Those*	Noun	Verb	
This	drawer	is	empty.	**These**	cabinets	are	for supplies.
That			for paper.	**Those**			locked.

2.2 Demonstratives Used Without Nouns

SINGULAR			PLURAL		
This / That	Verb		*These / Those*	Verb	
This	is	for you.	**These**	are	from your co-workers.
That		my desk.	**Those**		for us.

2.3 Using Demonstratives with Singular and Plural Nouns

a. Use *this* for a person or thing <u>near</u> you (a person or thing that is <u>here</u>).	**This** desk is Amanda's. **This** paper is for the printer.
b. Use *that* for a person or thing <u>not near</u> you (a person or thing that is <u>there</u>).	**That** desk is Janet's. **That** printer is a color printer.
c. Use *these* for people or things <u>near</u> you (people or things that are <u>here</u>).	**These** reports are for the meeting. **These** students are in your English class.
d. Use *those* for people or things <u>not near</u> you (people or things that are <u>there</u>).	**Those** folders are the sales reports. **Those** soccer players are great.
e. Use *this, that, these*, and *those* before nouns to identify and describe people and things.	**This photo** is my favorite. **That little girl** in the photo is my sister's daughter. **These charts** are helpful. **Those papers** are important.

2.4 Using Demonstratives with *Be*

a. You can use *this*, *that*, *these*, and *those* as pronouns to identify things.	**This is** the only copy machine. = *This copy machine is the only copy machine.* **That is** the color printer. = *That printer is the color printer.* **These are** the reports for the meeting. = *These reports are the reports for the meeting.* **Those are** my keys. = *Those keys are my keys.*
b. You can only use *this* and *these* as pronouns to introduce people.	A **This is** Claudia. B Hi, Claudia! Nice to meet you. A **These are** my co-workers, Mena and Liz. B Hello. Nice to meet you.
c. In informal speaking, use the contraction *that's* instead of *that is*.	**That's** a nice picture.

2.5 Questions with Demonstratives

a. To identify people, ask questions with *Who is . . . ?* If it's clear who you are talking about, you can omit the noun.	**Who is** that new teacher? **Who is** that?
b. To identify things, ask questions with *What is . . . ?* If it's clear what you are talking about, you can omit the noun.	**What is** that noise? **What is** that?
c. To ask about a price, use *How much is / are . . . ?* If it's clear what you are talking about, you can omit the noun.	**How much is** this printer? **How much is** this? **How much are** these printers? **How much are** these?
d. After questions with *this* and *that*, answer with *it* for things and *he* or *she* for people.	"How much is **this** copier?" "**It**'s $100." "Who is **that** lady?" "**She**'s my boss."
e. After questions with *these* and *those*, answer with *they*.	"Are **these** your reports?" "Yes, **they** are." "Who are **those** people?" "**They**'re my co-workers."

Exercise 2.1 Demonstratives with Singular and Plural Nouns

Help Margo describe her office. Write *this* or *these* for things that are near her, and *that* or *those* for things that are <u>not</u> near her.

1. ___*This*___ phone is new.

2. _____ closet is for her coat.

3. _____ books are about business.

4. _____ computer is old.

5. _____ pens are very good.

6. _____ window is open.

7. _____ papers are for the meeting.

8. _____ cabinet is for paper clips, folders, and general office things.

9. _____ picture is a photograph of her family.

10. _____ folders are for the sales reports.

Exercise 2.2 More Demonstratives with Singular and Plural Nouns

Pair Work What's in your pocket? What's in your bag? Tell your partner using *this* and *these*. Then your partner repeats everything using *that* and *those*.

A *This is a cell phone. These are keys. This is a pen. These are pencils. This is a paper clip.*

B *OK. That's a cell phone. Those are keys. That's a pen. Those are pencils. That's a paper clip.*

Exercise 2.3 Demonstratives Without Nouns

A Which noun isn't necessary? Cross out the noun. Check (✓) the sentences where you cannot cross out the noun.

Jane	How much are these (1) ~~memory sticks~~?
Salesclerk	$30.
Jane	Thank you. That's a nice (2) *computer*. ✓
Lisa	Yes, it has a big screen. What's that (3) *thing* on the front?
Salesclerk	It's the webcam. And here's the headphone jack.
Jane	Yeah. Is this (4) *model* a new model?
Salesclerk	No. This (5) *model* is an old model. That's why it's on sale. That's (6) *the new model* over there.
Jane	Oh, I see. Hey, these (7) *headphones* are great headphones.
Lisa	Yeah? Buy them!
Jane	Hmm . . . They're $250. No, thank you!

B ◀ᴼ)) Listen to the conversation and check your answers.

Exercise 2.4 Questions and Answers with Demonstratives

Circle the correct words.

1. *A* How much is **these /** ⟨**that**⟩ printer, please?   *B* ⟨**It's**⟩**/ They're** $220.
2. *A* Excuse me, how much are **these / this** scanners?   *B* **It's / They're** $150.
3. *A* How much is **those / this** electronic dictionary?   *B* **It's / They're** $100.
4. *A* Excuse me, how much are **that / those** pens?   *B* **It's / They're** $4.
5. *A* How much are **these / that** laptops?   *B* **It's / They're** on sale. **It's / They're** $300.
6. *A* How much is **those / that** digital photo frame?   *B* **It's / They're** $60.

Exercise 2.5 More Questions and Answers with Demonstratives

Pair Work Look around your classroom. In each box, write the names of three more things you see.

	Near Me	Not Near Me
Singular	*a desk, . . .*	*a map, . . .*
Plural	*books, . . .*	*windows, . . .*

Ask your partner *Yes/No* questions about the things above. Answer with *it* (singular) or *they* (plural).

A Is **that** a map of Iowa?

B No, **it**'s not. **It**'s a map of Illinois.

A Are **these** books new?

B Yes, **they** are.

Exercise 2.6 Vocabulary Focus: Responses with *That's*

You can use short responses with *That's* + adjective in conversations.	A I have a new job. B *That's* great! / *That's* good!		A My printer is broken. B *That's* too bad.	
Here are common adjectives to use with *that's*.	excellent OK	good terrible	great too bad	interesting wonderful	nice

Write a response with *That's* + adjective. Use the adjectives above.

1. It's a holiday tomorrow. *That's nice.*

2. We're on the same team! _____

3. Business isn't very good this year. _____

4. Patricia's not here today. She's sick. _____

5. I have a new laptop! _____

6. This cell phone has a dictionary. _____

3 Possessives and *Whose*

▶ Grammar Presentation

Possessives show that someone possesses (owns or has) something.	A *Is this **Diane's** desk?* B *No, it's **my** desk. **Her** desk is in the other office.* ***Her boss's** desk is in that office, too.*

3.1 *My, Your, His, Her, Its, Our, Their*

Subject	Possessive	
I	my	I'm not ready for class. **My** desk is very messy.
you	your	You are very organized. **Your** desk is so neat.
he	his	He is a new employee. **His** old job was in Hong Kong.
she	her	She isn't in the office now. **Her** computer is off.
it	its	It is a new company. **Its** president is Mr. Janesh.
we	our	We have the reports. **Our** boss wants to read them now.
you	your	You are co-workers. **Your** office is on the second floor.
they	their	They are at the office. **Their** boss is on vacation.

▸▸ Subject and Object Pronouns: See page A18.

3.2 Possessive Nouns

a. Add *'s* to singular nouns to show possession.	The ***manager's** name* (one manager) The ***boss's** ideas* (one boss)
b. Add an apostrophe (') to plural nouns ending in *-s* to show possession.	The ***managers'** names* (more than one manager) The ***bosses'** ideas* (more than one boss)
c. For irregular plural nouns, add *'s* to show possession.	The ***men's** books* (more than one man) The ***children's** room* (more than one child)
d. *My, your, his, her, our,* and *their* can come before a possessive noun.	***my friend's** job* ***our parents'** names*

▸▸ Capitalization and Punctuation Rules: See page A1.

3.3 *Whose?*

a. We can use *whose* to ask who owns something. We can use it with singular and plural nouns.	***Whose*** *jacket is this?* *I think that's **Kana's** jacket.*
b. We often use *whose* with *this, that, these,* and *those.*	***Whose*** *papers are **those**?* *Oh! They're **my** papers. Thank you.*

3.4 Using Possessives

a. Use the same possessive form before a singular noun or a plural noun.	**SINGULAR** ***my*** *friend* ***her*** *report* *the **boss's** report*	**PLURAL** ***my*** *friends* ***her*** *reports* *the **boss's** reports*
b. Use a possessive to show that someone owns something.	***her*** *pen **their** folders **Rachel's** car*	
c. Use a possessive to show that someone has something.	***your*** *name **my** birthday **Jared's** job*	
d. Use a possessive to show relationships between people.	***my*** *sister **his** boss **Claudia's** co-worker*	
e. Use a possessive noun to talk about places and countries.	*The **city's** population* ***Japan's** prime minister*	

▶ Grammar Application

Exercise 3.1 Possessives

Ben sends an e-mail to Dora and attaches some pictures. He describes them. Complete the e-mail. Use the possessive form of the pronoun in parentheses – *my, his, her, its, our, their* – or *'s*.

Hi Dora,

Here are the photos of __*our*__ (we) end-of-semester
(1)
party for _____ (we) English class. The first photo
(2)
is Juliana and Keiko. Is Juliana in _____ (you) math
(3)
5 class? She's sometimes _____ (I) partner in pair
(4)
work. Keiko is _____ (she) best friend.
(5)
Then, in the second photo, the woman in the
pink shirt is Sally. She's _____ (Juliana) sister.
(6)
_____ (They) family is in Chicago, but Sally is
(7)
10 here, too. The tall man is Mr. Donovan. He's
_____ (we) new teacher. _____ (He) first
(8)   (9)
name is Howard, and he's very friendly. In this photo
we're in the hall near _____ (Mr. Donovan) office.
(10)
Send me some pictures of your class.

15 Ben

Exercise 3.2 Possessive *'s* or *s'*?

A Circle the correct form of the possessive (*'s* or *s'*) in the sentences.

1. My **co-worker's** / **co-workers'** name is Krista.

2. **Krista's** / **Kristas'** last name is Logan.

3. She has two managers. Her **manager's** / **managers'** names are Tom and Sara.

4. **Sara's** / **Saras'** family is from Colombia.

5. She has two brothers. Her **brother's** / **brothers'** names are José and Carlos.

6. **Tom's / Toms'** wife is from New Jersey. Her name is Jessica.

7. Jessica and Tom have a daughter. Their **daughter's / daughters'** name is Danielle.

8. They have two cats. The **cat's / cats'** names are Sam and Max.

B *Pair Work* Tell a partner about someone you know at work or about a friend at school. Use the sentences in A as a model.

Exercise 3.3 Questions with *Whose* and *Who's*

A Complete the questions about the people in the photos with *Whose* and *Who's*. Then answer the questions.

Name: Ling Yang
Nationality: Chinese
Birthday: October 2
Best friend: Leila
Major: Nursing
Interests: yoga, art

Name: Ki-woon Do
Nationality: South Korean
Birthday: June 5
Best friend: Nora
Major: Business
Interests: soccer, movies

Name: Missolle Beauge
Nationality: Haitian
Birthday: April 7
Best friend: Lona
Major: Computers and Technology
Interests: music, cooking

1. _____Whose_____ best friend is Leila?   *Leila is Ling's best friend.*

2. _____ birthday is in June? _____

3. _____ Chinese? _____

4. _____ major is Business? _____

5. _____ Haitian? _____

6. _____ from South Korea? _____

7. _____ major is Nursing? _____

8. _____ birthday is in October? _____

9. _____ interested in soccer? _____

10. _____ interests are music and cooking? _____

B *Pair Work* Ask and answer other questions about the people in A.

A *Whose best friend is Nora?*
B *Nora is Ki-woon's best friend.*

A Complete the sentences. Use nationality adjectives.

1. Paula is from Brazil. She's _Brazilian_ .

2. My co-workers are from Chile. They're _____ .

3. Hakim is from Kuwait. He's _____ .

4. Alex is from Germany. He's _____ .

5. Vinh is from Vietnam. He's _____ .

6. Sarah is from England. She's _____ .

B *Over to You* Write three sentences about yourself. Then write sentences about three people from other countries. Remember to capitalize the names of countries and languages.

My name is Claudia. I'm from Mexico. I'm Mexican.

3 Questions with *What . . . like?* and *How* + Adjective

▶ Grammar Presentation

<table>
<tr>
<td>Questions with *What . . . like?* and *How* + adjective ask for a description. They are usually answered with an adjective.</td>
<td>A *"What is Arizona like?"*
B *"It's beautiful."*
A *"How deep is the Grand Canyon?"*
B *"It's very deep."*</td>
</tr>
</table>

3.1 Questions with *What . . . like?*

What + Be	Subject	Like	Answers with Adjectives
What is **What's**	New York	**like**?	It's **big**.
What are	the restaurants		They're **expensive**.

3.2 Questions with *How* + Adjective

How	Adjective	Be	Subject	Answers with Adjectives
How	**old**	is	the company?	It's 40 years **old**.
	tall	is	Jack?	He's 6 feet (1.80 meters) **tall**.
	long	are	the lines?	They're not **long**. They're very **short**.
	cold	is	the water?	It's not very **cold**. It's **warm**.

▶ Grammar Application

Exercise 3.1 Questions with *What . . . like?*

A Complete the conversation about the city of St. Louis. Use *What . . . like* in the questions. Then choose an answer from the box.

> It's very cold, and it's snowy.
> It's an old Midwestern city in Missouri.
>
> They're good and not too expensive.
> They're very friendly.

John I have exciting news! I have a new job!

Erica That's great!

John Well, the bad news is this: It's in St. Louis. It's not here in Chicago.

Erica Wow! <u>What's</u> St. Louis <u>like</u> ?
(1)　　　　　　　(1)

John _____
(2)

Erica _____ the weather _____
(3)　　　　　　　　　　　(3)
in the winter?

John _____
(4)

Erica _____ the people _____?
(5)　　　　　　　　　　(5)

John _____
(6)

Erica _____ the restaurants _____?
(7)　　　　　　　　　　　(7)

John _____
(8)

B 🔊 Listen to the conversation and check your answers.

C *Over to You* Write questions with *What . . . like in your city?* Then answer the questions with *It's* or *They're*.

1. (the weather) <u>*What's the weather like in your city? It's very hot in the summer.*</u>

2. (traffic) _____

3. (the people) _____

4. (the parks) _____

5. (the restaurants) _____

6. (the shopping) _____

Exercise 3.2 Questions with *How* + Adjective

A Complete these questions with *How* and an adjective from the box. Then ask and answer the questions with a partner.

A *How old is your city?*   *B* *It's really old. It's about 200 years old.*

bad	cold	crowded	expensive	hot	~~old~~

1. _____*How old*_____ is your city?
2. _____ is it in the summer?
3. _____ is it in the winter?
4. _____ is the downtown area with people?
5. _____ are the apartments?
6. _____ is the traffic?

B *Pair Work* Write six questions about a city to ask your partner. Write two with *What . . . like?* and three with *How* + adjective. Your partner chooses a city. Then you ask the questions and guess the city.

1. What *are winters like in this city?* _____
2. What _____
3. What _____
4. How _____
5. How _____
6. How _____
7. Let me guess. Is this city _____

4 Avoid Common Mistakes ⚠

1. An adjective can come before the noun it describes or after the verb *be*.

      long meeting   *is*
I have a ~~meeting long~~ every Wednesday. This meeting important.

2. Adjectives do not have plural forms.

      wonderful
I have three ~~wonderfuls~~ employees.

3. Use *an* before adjectives that begin with a vowel sound. Use *a* before adjectives that begin with a consonant sound.

     an   *a*
My sister is ~~a~~ ambitious person. She's ~~an~~ hardworking employee.

4. Nationality adjectives begin with a capital letter.

               Danish
Sven is from Denmark. He's ~~danish~~.

Editing Task

Find and correct nine more mistakes in these profiles from a social networking website.

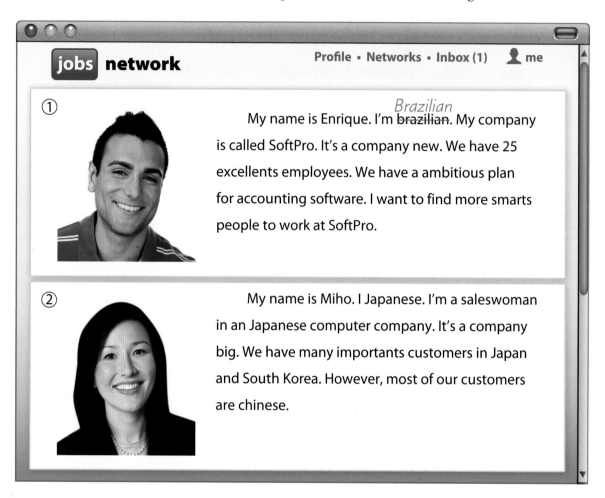

jobs network

Profile • Networks • Inbox (1) 👤 me

① My name is Enrique. I'm ~~brazilian~~ *Brazilian*. My company is called SoftPro. It's a company new. We have 25 excellents employees. We have a ambitious plan for accounting software. I want to find more smarts people to work at SoftPro.

② My name is Miho. I Japanese. I'm a saleswoman in an Japanese computer company. It's a company big. We have many importants customers in Japan and South Korea. However, most of our customers are chinese.

5 | Grammar for Writing ✎

Writing About Skills and Qualities

Writers use adjectives to describe their professional skills and their personal qualities. Remember:

- **Use adjectives before nouns and after *be* to describe the nouns.**
  Your boss is a <u>busy</u> person.   *Everyone in my office is <u>friendly</u>.*

- **Use *very* to make your statement stronger. But be careful not to use it too much, or the statements all become weaker.**
  My communication skills are <u>very</u> good.

Pre-writing Task

1 Read the paragraph below. How many qualities does the writer describe?

My Nursing Goal

My goal is to be a nurse for young children. I have a lot of useful qualities for nursing. I am a very friendly person. I love people, and I am very good with young children and small babies. I am also patient. I am a very hardworking person, and I am strong. My communication skills are good. I am smart. My science class grades are high. These qualities are very important for successful nurses.

2 Read the paragraph again. Circle the adjectives. Then draw an arrow from the adjectives to the nouns they describe. With which adjectives does the writer use *very*? Why?

Writing Task

1 *Write* Write about your ideal job. What are your professional skills and personal qualities? What makes you special for that job? Use the paragraph in the Pre-writing Task and the sentences below to help you write about your goal.

Use sentences such as:

- My goal is to be _____ (occupation).
- I have a lot of useful qualities for _____ (career).
- I am _____ (qualities).
- I am also a/an _____ person.

2 *Self-Edit* Use the editing tips below to improve your sentences. Make any necessary changes.

1. Did you use adjectives to write about your professional and personal skills and qualities?
2. Did you use both adjective + noun and *be* + adjective combinations?
3. Did you use *very* to make some of your statements stronger?
4. Did you avoid the mistakes in the Avoid Common Mistakes chart on page 59?

Prepositions

Around the House

1 Grammar in the Real World

A What's it like to have a houseguest? Maya is away, but her friend Cathy is her houseguest for the weekend. Read Maya's note to Cathy. Do you think Cathy is happy right now?

Hi Cathy,

    I'm happy you're **in** the apartment this weekend. My cat Fluffy is glad you're here, too. Please use my bedroom. Clean towels and sheets are **in** the closet. There's an extra blanket **in** the drawer **under** the bed.

5   I'm sorry the refrigerator's empty, but the supermarket's **across** the street. The car keys are **on top of** the refrigerator. The car's out of gas,[1] but the gas station's close, just two blocks away **on** Main Street.

    The TV's **in** the cabinet **near** the window. The remote control's **on** the counter **next**
10 **to** the coffee maker. (I think the batteries are dead. ☹)

    I'm sorry about the cat food **on** the floor. Fluffy's very messy. ☺ The vacuum cleaner's **in** the closet. It's old but it works.
15 The cleaning supplies are **behind** the plant. The garbage cans are **outside** the front door, **in front of** the garage.

    See you **on** Sunday evening. My bus arrives **at** 5:30 p.m. So expect me **between**
20 6:00 and 7:00.

Love,
Maya

P.S. I'm **at** my sister's house.
Her phone number is (212) 555-8749.

[1]**out of gas:** without gas

B *Comprehension Check* Match the two parts of the sentences about the note.

1. Maya is
2. The car is
3. The cat food is
4. Clean towels are
5. Cathy is

a. on the floor.
b. at her sister's house.
c. in the closet.
d. out of gas.
e. in the apartment.

C *Notice* Complete the sentences. Use the note to help you.

1. Clean towels and sheets are _____ the closet.
2. The car keys are _____ the refrigerator.
3. The remote control is _____ the counter _____ the coffee maker.
4. See you _____ Sunday evening.
5. My bus arrives _____ 5:30 p.m.

Which sentences tell you when something happens? Which sentences tell you where something is?

2 | Prepositions of Place: Things at Home and in the Neighborhood

▶ Grammar Presentation

Prepositions can show place. They can tell you where someone or something is.

*The remote control is **next to** the coffee maker.*
*My home is **near** the train station.*

2.1 Things at Home

in

*The vacuum cleaner is **in** the closet.*

under

*The shoes are **under** the bed.*

on / on top of

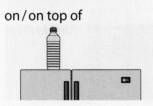

*The bottle is **on** the refrigerator.*

*The bottle is **on top of** the refrigerator.*

behind

*The cleaning supplies are **behind** the plant.*

2.1 Things at Home *(continued)*

above

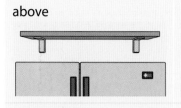

The shelf is **above** the refrigerator.

next to / near

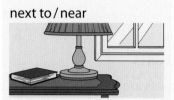

The book is **next to** the lamp.

The lamp is **near** the window.

in front of

The garbage can is **in front of** the garage.

between

The car keys are **between** the watch and the wallet.

2.2 Things in the Neighborhood

in front of

The man is **in front of** the bakery.

between

The bank is **between** the restaurant and the delicatessen.

behind

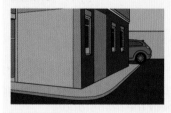

The car is **behind** the building.

across from

The woman is **across from** the bank.

next to / near

The coffee shop is **next to** the post office.

The coffee shop is **near** the bakery.

outside

The garbage can is **outside** the door.

at

The children are **at** the zoo.

inside

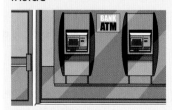

The ATMs are **inside** the bank.

▶ Grammar Application

Exercise 2.1 Prepositions of Place: Things at Home

A Complete the sentences with prepositions of place and the words in the box. Use the picture to help you. Sometimes more than one answer is possible.

| coffee maker | counter | door | floor | gym bag | refrigerator | table |

Sean I need my cell phone. Where is it?

Jon It's _on the table_ .
(1)

Sean Thanks. Now, where's my gym bag?

Jon It's _____ .
(2)

Sean OK. Oh, and I need my wallet. Where's that?

Jon It's _____ .
(3)

Sean And my keys. Where are my keys?

Jon They're _____ .
(4)

Sean Now, where's my laptop? I need my laptop.

Jon It's _____ .
(5)

Sean Is the newspaper outside the front door?

Jon No, it's _____ .
(6)

Sean And where are my books for school?

Jon They're _____ .
(7)

Sean Hey. How about a cup of coffee?

Jon Sure. Where's the coffee?

Sean It's _____ .
(8)

B Write questions with *Where* and answers. Use the picture in A to answer the questions.

1. (radio) _Where's his radio? It's on/on top of the refrigerator._

2. (watch) _____

3. (glasses) _____

4. (headphones) _____

5. (notebook) _____

C *Pair Work* Ask your partner about where things are in his or her home. Write six questions. Then answer your partner's questions. Use the words from the box.

bed	coffee maker	desk	remote control	sofa
clothes	computer	refrigerator	rug	

A *Where's your TV?*
B *It's in the living room. It's next to the bookshelf.*

Exercise 2.2 Prepositions of Place: Things in the Neighborhood

A Write sentences about the places in this neighborhood. Use four more of the prepositions from the box.

above	at	between	next to
across from	~~behind~~	in front of	outside

1. the gas station / the supermarket *The gas station is behind the supermarket.*

2. the camera store / the shoe store and the coffee shop _____

3. the red car / the gas station _____

4. the shopping carts / the supermarket _____

5. the bookstore / the bank _____

B ◄))) Listen. Where are these places? Write sentences. Use and reuse the prepositions from the box in A.

1. The parking lot is _in front of the supermarket._
2. The hair salon is _____
3. The movie theater is _____
4. The park is _____
5. The post office is _____

C *Pair Work* Ask and answer questions about your school and the area around the school.

A *Where's the post office?*   A *Is the school across from the bank?*
B *It's across from the school.*   B *No, it's next to the library.*

3 | Prepositions of Place: Locations and Other Uses

▶ Grammar Presentation

Certain prepositions commonly appear with some locations.	Maya's sister lives **in San Diego**. She lives **on Market Street**. Her home is **at 606 Market Street**.

3.1 *In*, *On*, and *At* with Locations

in + neighborhood . . . + city / town . . . + state . . . + country	*I live* **in Midtown**. *I live* **in Miami**. *My hometown is* **in Ohio**. *Montreal is* **in Canada**. **What state** *is Seattle* **in?**
on + street	*I live* **on Main Street**. *The restaurant is* **on Grand Avenue**. **What street** *is the movie theater* **on?**
at + address	*I live* **at 1298 Seventh Avenue**. *We met* **at 405 Broadway**.

3.2 Ordinal Numbers with Streets and Floors

1 first	7 seventh	13 thirteenth	19 nineteenth
2 second	8 eighth	14 fourteenth	20 twentieth
3 third	9 ninth	15 fifteenth	21 twenty-first
4 fourth	10 tenth	16 sixteenth	30 thirtieth
5 fifth	11 eleventh	17 seventeenth	31 thirty-first
6 sixth	12 twelfth	18 eighteenth	32 thirty-second

Use ordinal numbers with some streets.	*I live on **Third Avenue**.* *My apartment is on **Ninth Street**.*
Use *on* + *the* + ordinal number + *floor*.	*The doctor's office is **on the second floor**.* *I live **on the fifteenth floor**.*

3.3 Common Expressions with Prepositions

at home (*or* home)	*Maya is not **at home** this weekend.* NOT *Maya is not ~~at the home~~ this weekend.*
at work	*She is not **at work** today.* NOT *Maya is not ~~at the work~~ today.*
at school / college in school / college	*It's 10:30. Cathy's **at school** right now.* (= in the building) *I'm a student. I'm still **in school**.* (= still a student)
in class / in a meeting	*Tom is **in class**.* (= in the classroom)
on campus	*The bookstore is **on campus**.*
across the street	*The student center is **across the street**.*

▶ # Grammar Application

Exercise 3.1 *In, On,* and *At* with Locations

A *Pair Work* Complete the questions with the correct prepositions. Then write the full answers to the questions. Use your own ideas. Check your answers with a partner.

1. Are we _in_ Canada right now? _____

2. What town or city are we _____ ? _____

3. Are we still _____ Broad Street? _____

4. Are you _____ 25 Madison Avenue? _____

5. Are the restrooms _____ the first floor? _____

6. What street is this school _____ ? _____

B Complete the paragraphs about a student. Use *in*, *on*, or *at*.

My name is Blanca González, and I am from Mexico. My hometown is _*in*_ Mexico. Now I live _____ the United

(1)   (2)
States. I live _____ Waltham, Massachusetts. It's near

(3)
Boston. My apartment is _____ 399 Moody Street. My

(4)
parents also live in Waltham, _____ 147 Hope Avenue.

(5)
They are only two minutes away from my apartment.

I have three roommates. Our apartment is _____ the third floor. There is a

(6)
large supermarket _____ my street. There are also several gas stations _____ my

(7)   (8)
neighborhood. It's noisy _____ the street, but it's OK _____ our apartment. During

(9)   (10)
the day I study accounting. In the evenings I work at a restaurant _____ Watertown.

(11)
That's a town next to Waltham.

Exercise 3.2 *In, On,* and *At* with Locations and Ordinal Numbers

A *Over to You* Complete the information about your home and school. Use the information in parentheses.

1. My hometown is ____*in*____ ____*Illinois*____ .

     (preposition) (state or country)

2. My hometown is between _____ and _____ .

                (one city/town)   (another city/town)

3. Now I live _____ _____ .

   (preposition)   (neighborhood)

4. My home is _____ _____ .

   (preposition)   (street name)

5. I live _____ _____ .

  (preposition)   (address – You can give an imaginary address.)

6. My home is near _____ .

          (a place or building)

7. My classroom is _____ _____ _____ floor.

    (preposition) (+ *the*) (ordinal number)

8. My school is across the street from _____ .

               (a place)

B *Pair Work* Share your information with a partner.

Exercise 3.3 Expressions with *In, On,* and *At*

Complete the cell phone conversations. Use *in, on,* or *at.* Sometimes more than one answer is possible.

1. **Ashley** Hi, this is Ashley.

   Sarah Hi. This is Sarah. Where are you?

   Ashley I'm _at_ work. How about you? Are

   you _____ home?

   Sarah No, I'm _____ the movie

   theater _____ Fourth Street, and

   I'm cold.

   Ashley Oh, sorry. I'm late. I'm on my way.

2. **Rodrigo** Hi, it's me.

   Bob Hi. Where are you? Are you _____

   class?

   Rodrigo No. Class starts in two minutes.

   I'm _____ campus, but I think my

   backpack's _____ my closet.

   Can you bring it?

   Bob Sure. No problem. I'm still _____ the

   apartment.

3. **Alan** Hey. Where are you? Are you _____ class?

   Inga No. I'm _____ campus. Class starts in

   five minutes.

   Alan OK. I'm _____ home, but I'll be _____ work tonight.

   Inga OK, thanks for the reminder. I won't wait for you for dinner.

4. **Joseph** Mike? It's Joseph. Are you _____ school today?

   Mike Hi, Joseph. Yes. I'm _____ the library.

   Joseph Well, I'm _____ the coffee shop _____ Sullivan Street.

   Are you free?

   Mike Sure. See you in five minutes.

4 Prepositions of Time

▶ Grammar Presentation

Prepositions can tell you about when something happens.	Maya returns **on** Sunday. Her bus arrives **at** 5:30 p.m. Cathy expects her **between** 6:00 and 7:00.

4.1 *In, On, At*

Use *in* + parts of the day	Cathy always goes for a walk **in the afternoon**. On Mondays, I work **in the morning**.
Use *in* + month	My birthday is **in December**. Vietnam is beautiful **in April**.
Use *in* + season	Waltham is very cold **in the winter**. Please visit me **in the spring**.

People also say, for example, "in winter" and "in spring," but "in the winter" and "in the spring" are more common.

Use *on* + date In dates, write the number, but say the ordinal number.	I'll see you **on July 1**. My class ends **on May 20**.	(on July first) (on May twentieth)

People also say, for example, "the twentieth of May," but "May twentieth" is more frequent.

Use *on* + day	See you **on Monday**. Our class begins **on Friday**.	
Use *at* + specific time	The bank opens **at 7:00**. I usually wake up **at 5:30**.	(at seven / at seven o'clock) (at five-thirty / at half past five)

4.2 Questions with Days, Dates, and Times

You can ask questions about days, dates, or times with: *When is / are . . .* *What day is . . .* *What time is . . .* You can give shorter or longer answers to questions about days, dates, and times.	"**When is** Independence Day?" "It's on July 4. / On July 4. / July 4." "**What time is** your class?" "It's at 8:00. / At 8:00. / 8:00."

▶ Grammar Application

Exercise 4.1 *In, On, At* with Time

A Circle the correct preposition.

1. In my state, it's very cold **at** /**(in)** the winter and very hot **at** / **in** the summer.

2. The warm weather usually starts **on** / **in** April.

3. Unfortunately, it rains a lot **in** / **on** the spring.

4. The first day of summer is **in** / **on** June.

5. In the summer, the sun goes down late **at** / **in** the evening.

6. It's still sunny when I finish my class **on** / **at** 7:00.

7. I usually stay up late **on** / **in** Fridays and look at the stars.

8. I like to wake up **on** / **at** 6:30 on Saturdays because the weather is still cool **in** / **at** the morning.

Data from the Real World

People often give approximate times with *around* or *about*.	*See you around 6:30.* (= 6:20–6:40) *Call me about 6:15.* (= 6:10–6:20)
You can use *between* + two times.	*I'll see you between 6:00 and 7:00.*

B Complete the conversation. Use *in, on, at, around,* or *between*. Sometimes more than one answer is possible.

Alex Let's get together next week. Let's have lunch __on__ Monday.
　　　　　　　　　　　　　　　　　　　　　　　　　　(1)

　　　I'm free _____ 12:30 and 2:30.
　　　　　　　　　　(2)

Sam Monday? That's my brother's birthday. We always have lunch

　　　together _____ my brother's birthday.
　　　　　　　　　　(3)

Alex How about _____ Tuesday?
　　　　　　　　　　(4)

Sam Well, I have class _____ the afternoon on Tuesday.
　　　　　　　　　　　　　(5)

　　　It's _____ 1:00. It usually finishes _____ 2:15.
　　　　　(6)　　　　　　　　　　　　　　　　　　(7)

　　　Let's meet _____ Wednesday.
　　　　　　　　　　(8)

Alex Great. Let's meet _____ Wednesday then,
　　　　　　　　　　　　　　(9)

　　　_____ 1:00.
　　　　(10)

C *Over to You* Write six sentences about dates that are special for you. Then share your sentences with a partner.

My mother's birthday is on July 16. My favorite holiday is Independence Day. It's on July 4.

Exercise 4.2 Questions with Days, Dates, and Times

A Unscramble the words to make questions about the Expo.

1. the / Expo / is / When

   When is the Expo?

2. day / What / is / the concert

   _____

3. the students / do / a break / When / have

   _____

4. the Career Fair / What / is / day

   _____

5. is / lunch / When

   _____

6. the welcome / is / time / What

   _____

VALE COMMUNITY COLLEGE

Music Industry Expo
Thursday, April 22, 7 p.m.–10 p.m.

Concert
Friday, April 23, 9 a.m.–5 p.m.

———————— Friday ————————

9:00 Welcome
9:30 "The Business of Music"
10:30 "Becoming a Songwriter"
11:15–11:30 Break
11:30 Talk by Sound Engineer
12:30–1:30 Lunch
1:30 "Writing Music for the Movies"
2:30–4:30 Career Fair
4:30 New Music Software

B *Pair Work* Ask and answer the questions in A with a partner.

A *When is the Expo?*
B *It's on Thursday, April 22.*

5 | Avoid Common Mistakes ⚠

1. Use *in* + month, but use *on* + date or day.

    on   *in*   *on*
My birthday is ~~in~~ May 10. My sister's birthday is ~~on~~ May, too, but it's not ~~in~~ the same day.

2. Use *at* + time.

       at
My bus arrives ∧9:00.

3. Use *on* + street name. Use *at* + address.

    on   *at*
My house is ~~in~~ Gorge Avenue. It's ~~on~~ 1276 Gorge Avenue.

4. Use *on* + *the* + ordinal number + *floor*.

    on the
My office is ~~in~~ third floor.

Editing Task

Find and correct nine more mistakes in this e-mail about a birthday celebration.

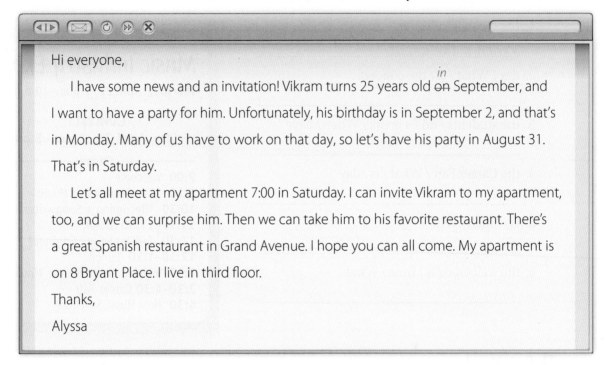

Hi everyone,

    I have some news and an invitation! Vikram turns 25 years old ~~on~~ *in* September, and I want to have a party for him. Unfortunately, his birthday is in September 2, and that's in Monday. Many of us have to work on that day, so let's have his party in August 31. That's in Saturday.

    Let's all meet at my apartment 7:00 in Saturday. I can invite Vikram to my apartment, too, and we can surprise him. Then we can take him to his favorite restaurant. There's a great Spanish restaurant in Grand Avenue. I hope you can all come. My apartment is on 8 Bryant Place. I live in third floor.

Thanks,

Alyssa

6 | Grammar for Writing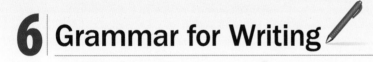

Using Prepositions

Writers use prepositions of place and time when they write invitations. Remember:

- **The prepositions *in*, *on*, and *at* have many different meanings.**

  The party is <u>on</u> the ninth.   My house is <u>on</u> Kellogg Street.   The invitation is <u>on</u> the kitchen counter.

- **A lot of prepositions are two or more words.**

  I live <u>next to</u> Surma.   The bus stop is <u>in front of</u> the bank.

Pre-writing Task

1 Read the e-mail invitation. What is it an invitation for? When is the party? Where is the party?

> Hi Raul,
>
> You're invited(to)a graduation party for Claudia at my house on Saturday, the ninth. The party is at 6:00 p.m. I have a new apartment. It's at 616 Campana Way. My apartment is on the third floor. My building doesn't have a parking lot. You can park in the parking lot behind the bank. The bank is across from the gas station on Kellogg Street.
>
> See you soon!
> Daniel

2 Read the e-mail invitation again. Circle all the prepositions. Then complete the top of the invitation.

What: _____

When: _____

Where: _____

Writing Task

1 *Write* Write an e-mail invitation to a special party. What is the reason for the party? Where is the party? When is the party? Where is parking, or where is a bus stop near the party? Use the e-mail in the Pre-writing Task to help you. Use prepositions of place and time from the unit.

2 *Self-Edit* Use the editing tips below to improve your sentences. Make any necessary changes.

  1. Did you use time and location prepositions in your e-mail invitation?
  2. Did you use *in*, *on*, and *at* correctly?
  3. Did you use any prepositions that are two or three words?
  4. Did you avoid the mistakes in the Avoid Common Mistakes chart on page 73?

There Is and *There Are*

Local Attractions

1 | Grammar in the Real World

A Do you know a lot about the old areas of your town? Read the blog about a historic street in Los Angeles. What are some fun things to do there?

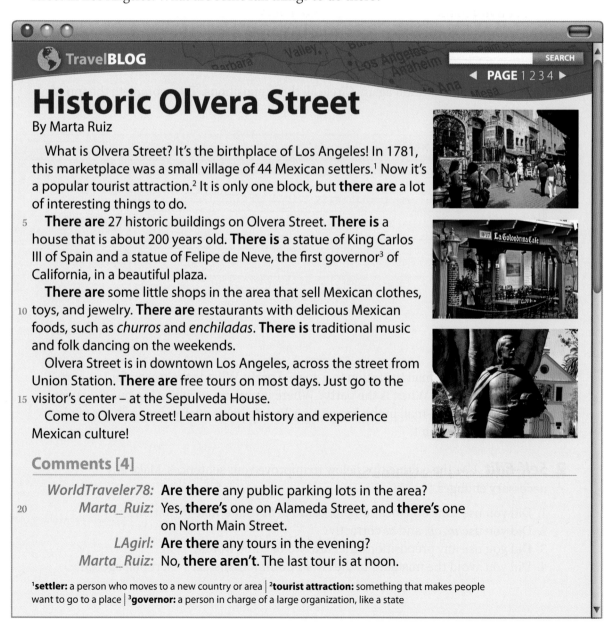

TravelBLOG

SEARCH

◀ **PAGE** 1 2 3 4 ▶

Historic Olvera Street

By Marta Ruiz

What is Olvera Street? It's the birthplace of Los Angeles! In 1781, this marketplace was a small village of 44 Mexican settlers.[1] Now it's a popular tourist attraction.[2] It is only one block, but **there are** a lot of interesting things to do.

5 **There are** 27 historic buildings on Olvera Street. **There is** a house that is about 200 years old. **There is** a statue of King Carlos III of Spain and a statue of Felipe de Neve, the first governor[3] of California, in a beautiful plaza.

There are some little shops in the area that sell Mexican clothes,
10 toys, and jewelry. **There are** restaurants with delicious Mexican foods, such as *churros* and *enchiladas*. **There is** traditional music and folk dancing on the weekends.

Olvera Street is in downtown Los Angeles, across the street from Union Station. **There are** free tours on most days. Just go to the
15 visitor's center – at the Sepulveda House.

Come to Olvera Street! Learn about history and experience Mexican culture!

Comments [4]

WorldTraveler78:	**Are there** any public parking lots in the area?
20 *Marta_Ruiz:*	Yes, **there's** one on Alameda Street, and **there's** one on North Main Street.
LAgirl:	**Are there** any tours in the evening?
Marta_Ruiz:	No, **there aren't**. The last tour is at noon.

[1]**settler:** a person who moves to a new country or area | [2]**tourist attraction:** something that makes people want to go to a place | [3]**governor:** a person in charge of a large organization, like a state

B Comprehension Check Match the two parts of the sentences about Olvera Street.

1. Olvera Street was	a. little shops in the area.
2. It's a tourist attraction	b. interesting things to do.
3. There are a lot of	c. at noon.
4. There are some	d. in downtown Los Angeles.
5. The last tour is	e. a small village in 1781.

C Notice Find these words in the text. Do they come after *there is* or *there are*? Write the words in the correct columns.

a lot of interesting things to do	27 historic buildings	a statue of King Carlos III
traditional music	restaurants	

There is . . .	There are . . .

Now circle the correct words in these two sentences about *there is* and *there are*.

The writer uses **_There is_ / _There are_** with singular nouns. She uses **_There is_ / _There are_** with plural nouns.

2 There Is / There Are

▶ Grammar Presentation

There is and *There are* tell you that something or someone exists or that something is a fact.	**There's** *a statue of King Carlos III in this plaza.* **There are** *free tours on most days.*

2.1 Affirmative Statements

There	Be	Subject	Place / Time		Contraction
There	**is**	a parking lot a free tour	on Alameda Street. at 10:00.		There is → There's
	are	some little shops free tours	in the area. on most days.		

2.2 Negative Statements

There	Be + Not/No	Subject	Place/Time
There	**isn't**	a bank	in Union Station.
	is no	bank	
	isn't	a show	at 8:00.
	is no	show	
	's no	bank	in Union Station.
		show	at 8:00.
	aren't	any cars	on Olvera Street.
	are no	cars	
	aren't	any tours	in the evening.
	are no	tours	

2.3 Using *There Is / There Are*

a. Use *There is / There are* to say that something or someone exists or to introduce a fact or a situation.

> **There are** *a lot of interesting things to do in this area.*
> **There's** *an article by Marta Ruiz on this website.*
> **There are** *two questions from readers.*

b. Use *There is / There are* to tell the location of something or someone.

> **There's** *a parking lot on the corner.*
> **There are** *some Mexican restaurants on the next block.*
> **There's a** *tour guide at the door.*

c. Use *There is / There are* to tell when an event happens.

> **There's** *an art show at 8:00.*
> **There are** *concerts on the weekend.*

d. Use the full forms in academic writing, but in speaking, use contractions.

> **There's** *music in the plaza.*
> **There's** *no free parking on this street.*

In informal speech, people often say *There're* instead of *There are*, but don't write it.

> **There are** *a lot of museums in Los Angeles.*
> NOT ~~**There're**~~ *a lot of museums in Los Angeles.*

e. Use *There is* when there are two or more nouns and the first noun is singular.

> SINGULAR NOUN   PLURAL NOUN
> **There's** *a jewelry store and two restaurants on this street.*

Use *There are* when there are two or more nouns and the first noun is plural.

> PLURAL NOUN   SINGULAR NOUN
> **There are** *two restaurants and a jewelry store on this street.*

f. You can use *some* with a plural noun after *There are*.

> **There are some** *shops around the corner.*

2.3 Using *There Is* / *There Are* (continued)

g. For negative statements, you can use *There isn't* and *There aren't*. The full forms *is not* and *are not* are not often used.	***There isn't*** a bad restaurant on this street. ***There aren't*** any parking spaces here.
OR You can use *There is* / *There are* + *no*.	***There's no*** fee at this parking lot. ***There are no*** hotels around here.
You can use *any* in negative statements with *There aren't*.	***There aren't any*** traffic lights on Olvera Street.
h. You can use *There is* and *There are* to introduce new people, places, and things.	INTRODUCTION MORE INFORMATION ***There is*** an old house on the street. ***It's*** now a museum.
You can use *It is* / *It's* and *They are* / *They're* to give more information.	***There are*** a lot of shops on Olvera. ***They are*** all very nice.

▶ Grammar Application

Exercise 2.1 Affirmative Statements

A Complete the sentences from an e-mail. Use *There's* or *There are*.

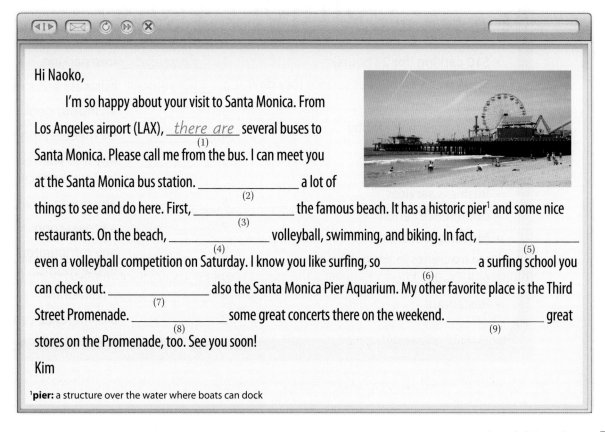

Hi Naoko,

I'm so happy about your visit to Santa Monica. From Los Angeles airport (LAX), <u>*there are*</u> several buses to
(1)
Santa Monica. Please call me from the bus. I can meet you at the Santa Monica bus station. _____ a lot of
(2)
things to see and do here. First, _____ the famous beach. It has a historic pier[1] and some nice
(3)
restaurants. On the beach, _____ volleyball, swimming, and biking. In fact, _____
(4)   (5)
even a volleyball competition on Saturday. I know you like surfing, so_____ a surfing school you
(6)
can check out. _____ also the Santa Monica Pier Aquarium. My other favorite place is the Third
(7)
Street Promenade. _____ some great concerts there on the weekend. _____ great
(8)   (9)
stores on the Promenade, too. See you soon!

Kim

[1]**pier:** a structure over the water where boats can dock

B *Over to You* What is your favorite city? Fill in the chart with some of the interesting places in your favorite city.

There is . . .	There are . . .

C *Pair Work* Tell your partner what is in your favorite city. Use your information from B. Take turns.

A There's an art museum.
B There are several big parks.

Exercise 2.2 Affirmative and Negative Statements

A Look at the hotel information. Complete the sentences. Use *There is / are* and *There isn't / aren't*.

Comfort Hotel

- $10 parking (for 24 hours)
- $7.95 wireless Internet service (per day)
- Free breakfast
- Free coffee in the lobby
- Outdoor pool
- Fitness room
- Business services
- Conference center
- Meeting rooms (4)
- Ice machines in the hallways
- Park views
- Restaurant

1. ___*There isn't*___ free parking.
2. ___*There are*___ business services.
3. _____ an indoor pool.
4. _____ six meeting rooms.
5. _____ any free wireless Internet service.
6. _____ any ocean views.
7. _____ a fitness room.
8. _____ any refrigerators in the rooms.
9. _____ a restaurant.
10. _____ a conference center.

B *Over to You* What doesn't exist in your town or city? Look at the places in the box. Add your own ideas. Write six sentences about your town or city. Use *There is no* and *There aren't any*.

aquarium	cheap restaurants	historic houses	park	statues
beach	free parking	library	public pool	tourist attractions
bus station	gas stations	museums	river	train station

1. *There aren't any gas stations.* _____
2. _____
3. _____
4. _____
5. _____
6. _____
7. _____

Exercise 2.3 *There Is / There Are* or *It Is / They Are*

A Read Mi-Sun's description of her town on her blog. Complete the sentences. Use *There's*, *There are*, *It's*, or *They're*.

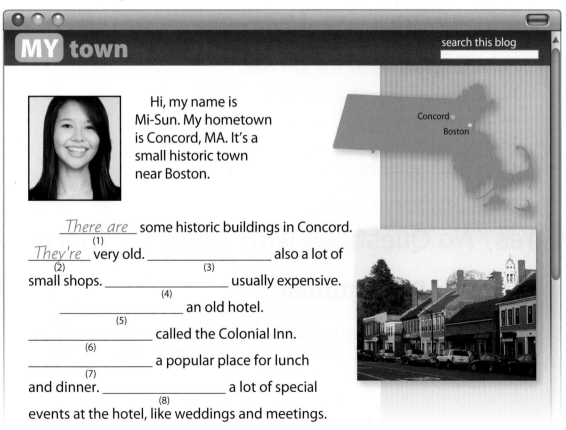

MY town   search this blog

Hi, my name is Mi-Sun. My hometown is Concord, MA. It's a small historic town near Boston.

There are some historic buildings in Concord.
(1)
They're very old. _____ also a lot of
(2)   (3)
small shops. _____ usually expensive.
(4)
_____ an old hotel.
(5)
_____ called the Colonial Inn.
(6)
_____ a popular place for lunch
(7)
and dinner. _____ a lot of special
(8)
events at the hotel, like weddings and meetings.

Concord
Boston

_____ often live music at night. I like
(9)
to go and listen to jazz.

_____ a national park by the
(10)
Concord River. _____ beautiful
(11)
and peaceful. _____ always lots of
(12)
tourists at the park. It has a famous bridge – Old
North Bridge. Also, _____ a very
(13)
famous statue of a minuteman next to the bridge.
The soldier was called a "minuteman" because
he could get ready in a minute. A historic battle
happened there in 1775. I often walk there
with friends.

B 🔊 Listen to Mi-Sun and check your answers.

C *Over to You* Write four pairs of sentences about your town or city. Use *There's / There are* in the first sentence. Use *It's* or *They are* in the second sentence to add more information.

There's a big park in my city. It's on State Street.

1. _____
2. _____
3. _____
4. _____

3 | Yes / No Questions with *There Is / There Are*

▶ Grammar Presentation

Yes / No Questions with *There is / There are* can ask about people, things, and events.	**Is there** a tour guide in this museum? **Are there** any concerts on Friday?

3.1 *Yes / No* Questions and Short Answers

Be	*There*	Subject	Place / Time	Short Answers
Is	**there**	a visitor's center	on Olvera Street?	Yes, **there is**.
		a performance	at 6:00?	No, **there isn't**.
Are		any parking lots	in the area?	Yes, **there are**.
		any tours	in the evening?	No, **there aren't**.

3.2 Using *Yes / No* Questions and Short Answers with *There Is / There Are*

a. You can use *any* with a plural noun in *Yes / No* questions with *Are there*.	**"Are there any** hotels on Alameda Street?" **"Are there any** concerts on weekdays?"
b. In affirmative short answers, don't use the contractions *there's* or *there're*.	"Yes, **there is**." NOT "Yes, ~~there's~~." "Yes, **there are**." NOT "Yes, ~~there're~~."
c. You can use *It is / They are* to say more after a short answer.	"Is there a visitor's center on Olvera Street?" "Yes, there is. **It is** at the Sepulveda House." "Are there any parking lots in the area?" "Yes, there are. **They are** on Alameda Street."

3.3 Longer Answers with *There Is / There Are*

a. In longer answers with *There is*, you can use *one* instead of repeating *a* + singular noun.	*Is there a visitor's center on Olvera Street?* *Yes, there's* **one** *in the Sepulveda House.* *No, there isn't* **one** *on Olvera Street.*
b. In longer answers with *There are*, you can use *some / any* instead of repeating *some / any* + plural noun.	*Are there any public parking lots in the area?* *Yes, there are* **some** *on Alameda Street.* *No, there aren't* **any** *in the area.*

▶ Grammar Application

Exercise 3.1 Yes/No Questions and Answers

A Read the TV schedule and complete the questions and answers. Use *Are there any* and *Is there a* for the questions. Then write short answers.

T.V. tonight			Page 5
6:30 p.m.	News: *Weather report*	11:15 p.m.	Movie: *Where Is Jimmy Jones?*
7:00 p.m.	Talk show: *The Guy Norris Show*	1:00 a.m.	Music: *The Dixonville Festival*
8:00 p.m.	Documentary: *Antarctica*	2:00 a.m.	Music: *Jazz with Kenny Delmot*
9:00 p.m.	Movie: *The Long Road*	3:00 a.m.	Comedy: *The Watson Family*

1. __*Are there any*__ movies on TV tonight? Yes, there _____ two movies. There's one at 9:00 and one at 11:15.

2. __*Is there a*__ talk show? Yes, _____ one at 7:00.

3. _____ music shows? Yes, there _____ . There's one at _____ and one at _____ .

4. _____ sports shows? _____.

5. _____ documentary? _____ one at 8:00.

6. _____ kids' show? _____.

7. _____ comedy show? _____.

8. _____ news program? _____.

B *Pair Work* Write questions about events in your city or town. Use *Is there a/an* and *Are there any*. Then ask and answer the questions with a partner. Write the answers to the questions with your partner.

A *Are there any good movies this weekend?*
B *Yes, there are two good movies.*

1. (art festival) _____

2. (jazz concerts) _____

3. (baseball game) _____

4. (dance performance) _____

5. (new paintings at the museum) _____

6. (good movies) _____

C Answer each question with *yes* in three different ways. Give information about your own area, if possible.

1. Is there a mall in this town?

   Yes, there's one on Westwood Avenue. Yes, there's a mall on Westwood Avenue.
   Yes, it's on Westwood Avenue.

2. Is there a good coffee shop nearby?

   _____

3. Is there an art museum?

   _____

4. Is there a nice park?

   _____

5. Is there a sports stadium?

   _____

6. Is there a big movie theater?

   _____

4 Avoid Common Mistakes ⚠

1. Use *There is* with singular nouns. Use *There are* with plural nouns.

         is   *are*
There ~~are~~ a music festival this week.   There ~~is~~ musicians from different countries at the festival.

2. *There is* and *There are* introduce <u>new</u> people, places, and things. *It is* and *They are* give more information.

                                             It
There is a small building on Thomas Street. ~~There~~ is the town museum.
There
~~They~~ are three large cities in Texas. They are Houston, San Antonio, and Dallas.

3. Use the full forms in academic writing. Do not use the contractions.

There is
~~There's~~ a wonderful museum in downtown Philadelphia.
There is
~~There's~~ no bank in the train station.

4. In informal speaking, people often say *There are* very quickly, so it sounds like *They're*. Don't confuse them in writing.

There are
~~They're~~ some great shows this weekend.

Editing Task

Find and correct seven more mistakes in this article about New York City's famous park.

New York City's Central Park

$\qquad$New York City is an expensive place to visit, but there ~~are~~ ^{IS} one place that is always

free: Central Park. There is a very big park. In fact, it is about 2.5 miles (4 km) long

and 0.5 miles (0.8 km) wide. There is over 843 acres[1] in the park. There is fields, ponds,

and lakes. Visitors enjoy different kinds of sports and events here. There are walkers,

5 joggers, skaters, bicyclists, and bird-watchers. There are a zoo and two ice-skating

rinks. There's also an outdoor theater.

The theater has "Shakespeare in the Park"

summer festivals. There is a swimming pool

in the summer, too. Throughout the year,

10 they're horse-and-carriage rides. Every year,

there is over 25 million visitors. They are

happy to visit a fun and free New York City

tourist attraction.

[1] **843 acres:** 1.32 square miles or 3.41 square kilometers

5 | Grammar for Writing

Writing About Places

Writers use *There is* and *There are* when they describe places.
Remember:

- **You can follow *There is / There are* sentences with *It is / They are* sentences. These sentences give more information.**
  There are some mountains near my town. They are very tall.

- **Use *some* in affirmative statements and *any* or *no* in negative statements.**
  There are some big trees near my house.   *There are not any buses on my street. There are no traffic lights.*

Pre-writing Task

1 Read the paragraph below. What kind of place does the writer describe? What is in the place?

Elwood Park

There is a big park near my apartment. It is very beautiful. There is a playground in the park. It always has a lot of children. There are also some small lakes. One lake is for swimming. It has a little beach. The other lakes do not have any beaches. They are for fishing. There are some small boats to rent. There is a fountain in the center of the park. It is a very cool place to be in the summer. There are not any food stands, but there are a lot of picnic tables.

2 Read the paragraph again. Underline *There* and circle the pronouns *It* and *They*. Draw an arrow from the *It* and *They* pronouns to the nouns that they refer to.

Writing Task

1 *Write* Use the paragraph in the Pre-writing Task to help you write about a place that you like. Where is this place? What is in it? What is missing? What is special about the place? You can write about:

- a park
- a neighborhood in your town or city
- a street in your town or city
- the downtown or city center

- a museum
- a special building
- a beach or hill near your home
- your school or place of work

Use sentences such as:

- There are _____ . They are _____ .
- There is _____ . It is _____ .
- There is / are not any _____ .
- There are some _____ .

2 *Self-Edit* Use the editing tips below to improve your sentences. Make any necessary changes.

1. Did you use *There is / There are* sentences to describe a place?
2. Did you use *It is / They are* sentences to give more information?
3. Did you use *some* with affirmative statements and *any* or *no* with negative statements?
4. Did you avoid the mistakes in the Avoid Common Mistakes chart on page 85?

Simple Present
Lifestyles

1 | Grammar in the Real World

A Is there someone very old in your family? Read the magazine article about places where people live a long time. Why do some people have a long life?

A Long, Healthy Life

On the Japanese island of Okinawa, many people **live** to be over 100 years old. Researchers[1] **find** this in several places around the world, including Sardinia, Italy; Icaria, Greece; the Nicoya Peninsula of Costa Rica; and Loma Linda, California. Why do people in these areas **live** so long? The answer **is** lifestyle.[2] This list **shows** six lifestyle habits[3] that **are** common in these places.

1. People in these areas **move** around a lot. They **don't exercise** in a gym, but they **walk** a lot during the day. They **use** their bodies and **live** actively.
2. They **have** a purpose in their lives. Some **spend** time with grandchildren. Others **do** gardening or volunteer work.[4]
3. They **relax**. **Every day**, they **take** time to rest and relax. They **rarely feel** stressed.[5]
4. They **eat** lots of vegetables, and they **usually don't eat** meat.
5. They **have** many friends. They **are** part of an active social group.
6. They **feel** close to their families.

[1]**researcher:** a person who studies something to learn detailed information about it | [2]**lifestyle:** the way people live; how people eat, sleep, work, exercise | [3]**habit:** something you do or the way you act regularly | [4]**volunteer work:** work without pay, usually to help other people or an organization | [5]**stressed:** very nervous or worried

B *Comprehension Check* Answer the questions.

1. Why do people in some areas live so long?
2. Do these people feel stressed?
3. Do they eat much meat?

C *Notice* Find the sentences in the article. Complete the sentences with the correct words.

1. People in these areas ___ *move* ___ around a lot.
2. They ___ *don't* ___ exercise in a gym.
3. They ___ *walk* ___ a lot during the day.
4. ___ *Every day* ___ , they ___ *take* ___ time to rest and relax.

Find the places you use *don't*. What words show time?

2 | Simple Present: Affirmative and Negative Statements

▶ Grammar Presentation

The simple present describes habits, routines, and facts.	*In some cultures, people **live** to be 100 years old. These people **exercise** and **eat** very well.*

2.1 Affirmative Statements

SINGULAR			PLURAL		
Subject	Verb		Subject	Verb	
I You	**eat**	vegetables every day.	We You They	**eat**	vegetables every day.
He She It	**eats**				

2.2 Negative Statements

SINGULAR				PLURAL			
Subject	Do / Does + Not	Base Form of Verb		Subject	Do + Not	Base Form of Verb	
I You	do not don't	eat	a lot of meat.	We You They	do not don't	exercise	in the morning.
He She It	does not doesn't						

2.3 Using Simple Present and Time Expressions

a. Use simple present to talk about things that regularly happen, such as habits and routines.	*Okinawans usually **eat** fruits and vegetables.* *We **don't eat** meat.* *He **doesn't drive** to work.*
b. When you talk about things that regularly happen, use time expressions such as *every day*, *every* + day, *in the morning / afternoon / evening*, *at night*, and *at 6:30*.	*They take long walks **every day**.* *She takes long walks **every Saturday**.* *We take naps **in the afternoon**.* *I watch TV **at night**.* *Our family eats dinner **at 6:30**.*
An *-s* after the day of the week / *morning / afternoon / evening* or *weekend* means the action or event always happens.	***On Saturdays**, I work in a restaurant.* *I take long walks **on weekends**.*
Use *from . . . to . . .* to say how long something happens.	*I work **from** 8:00 **to** 5:00.*
c. Time expressions usually come at the end of the sentence. If the time expression is at the beginning of the sentence, use a comma after it.	*I visit my grandparents **in the summer**.* ***In the summer**, I visit my grandparents.* ***In June**, I take a break from school.*
d. You can also use the simple present to talk about facts.	*Okinawans **live** long lives.*

2.4 Spelling Rules for Adding *-s*, *-es*, and *-ies* to Verbs

a. Add *-s* to most verbs. Add *-s* to verbs ending in a vowel[1] + *-y*.	*drinks, rides, runs, sees, sleeps* *buys, pays, says*
b. Add *-es* to verbs ending in *-ch, -sh, -ss, -x*. Add *-es* to verbs ending in a consonant[2] + *-o*.	*teaches, pushes, misses, fixes* *does, goes*
c. For verbs that end in a consonant + *-y*, change the *y* to *i* and add *-es*.	*cry* → *cries* *study* → *studies*
d. Some verbs are irregular.	*be* → *am / are / is* *have* → *has*

Reminder:
[1]Vowels: the letters *a, e, i, o, u*
[2]Consonants: the letters *b, c, d, f, g, h, j, k, l, m, n, p, q, r, s, t, v, w, x, y, z*
▸▸ Spelling and Pronunciation Rules for Simple Present: See page A20.

Data from the Real World

Here are some of the most frequent simple present verbs:

be	do	get	know	see	come	want
have	say	go	think	make	take	give

▶ Grammar Application

Exercise 2.1 Simple Present Statements

Complete the sentences with the correct form of the verbs in parentheses.

1. My grandparents _live_ (live) healthy lifestyles.

2. My grandfather ___goes___ (go) for a walk every morning.

3. In the afternoon, he ___checks___ (check) his e-mail and ___works___ (work) in his garden.

4. My grandmother ___is___ (be) also active.

5. She ___works___ (work) part-time in a hotel.

6. She ___does___ (do) volunteer work at a local school three days a week.

7. Before dinner, they ___relax___ (relax) in the living room.

8. They ___eat___ (eat) healthy food, and they ___not smoke___ (not smoke).

Exercise 2.2 More Simple Present Statements

Complete the statements with the affirmative or negative form of the verbs in parentheses.

1. Tran and his roommate, Edgar, _have_ (have) a lot to do every week.

2. They often ___feel___ (feel) stressed during the week.

3. Tran ___works___ (work) long hours at a department store.

4. He _doesn't see_ (not see) his family very much.

5. Tran and Edgar both ___take___ (take) night classes at the community college.

6. They usually _don't have_ (not have) time to cook dinner.

7. For dinner, they often ___eat___ (eat) fast food like hamburgers and French fries.

8. Edgar _doesn't have_ (not have) a job.

9. Every morning, he ___goes___ (go) online to look at job listings.

10. Edgar usually ___runs___ (run) in the afternoon.

11. On the weekends, Edgar and Tran ___relax___ (relax) with friends.

Exercise 2.3 More Simple Present Statements

A *Over to You* Complete the sentences about yourself. Use affirmative or negative forms of the verbs in the box.

do	eat	feel	live	sleep
drink	exercise	have	read	spend

1. I _don't feel_ stressed during the week.

2. I ___have___ good friends in my town.

3. I ___live___ very actively.

4. I ___exercise___ in a gym.

5. I _don't eat_ a lot of meat.

6. I ___sleep___ about eight hours every night.

7. I ___spend___ a lot of time online or on the computer.

8. I _don't do_ volunteer work in my area.

9. I ___drink___ a lot of water every day.

10. I _don't read_ the newspaper in the morning.

B *Pair Work* Share your sentences with a partner. Then change partners. Tell your new partner about your classmate.

> A *Ari feels stressed during the week.*
> B *Maria doesn't feel stressed during the week.*

Exercise 2.4 ◄》 Pronunciation Focus: -s and -es

Say /s/ after /f/, /k/, /p/, and /t/ sounds.	*laughs, drinks, walks, sleeps, writes, gets*
Say /z/ after /b/, /d/, /g/, /v/, /m/, /n/, /l/, and /r/ sounds and all vowel sounds.	*grabs, rides, hugs, lives, comes, runs, smiles, hears, sees, plays, buys, goes, studies*
Say /əz/ after /tʃ/, /ʃ/, /s/, /ks/, /z/, and /dʒ/ sounds.	*teaches, pushes, kisses, fixes, uses, changes*
Pronounce the vowel sound in *does* and *says* differently from *do* and *say*.	*do* /duː/ → *does* /dʌz/ *say* /seɪ/ → *says* /sez/

A ◄》 Listen and repeat the verbs in the chart above.

B Read about Staci's week. Underline the verbs that end in *-s* or *-es*.

    Staci goes to school from Monday to Friday from 7:30 a.m. to 11:30 a.m. Then she rushes to work. She works at a hospital until 8:00 p.m. In the evening, Staci catches a bus to go home. On her way home, she listens to music and relaxes. She eats a quick dinner with her family. Then she reads to her children and checks their homework. If she isn't too tired, she finishes her own homework. Staci usually falls asleep by 10:00 p.m.

C ◄)) Listen to the information about Staci's week and check (✓) the sounds of the verbs in the boxes below. Then practice saying the verbs.

	/s/	/z/	/əz/
1. goes		✓	
2. rushes			✓
3. works	✓		
4. catches			✓
5. listens	✓		
6. relaxes			
7. eats			
8. reads			
9. checks			
10. finishes			
11. falls			

D *Pair Work* Ask and answer the questions with a partner. Then tell the class about your partner.

I like swimming.

1. What are two of your healthy habits? *I go to a gym two times a week.*
2. What do you do to relax? *I watch movies, reading books, walking*

Paulo eats healthy food, and he doesn't smoke or drink. To relax, he listens to music.

Exercise 2.5 Using Time Expressions with Simple Present

	Sunday	Monday	Tuesday	Wednesday	Thursday	Friday	Saturday
Morning	Off	Get up 6:30 a.m. Work 7:30 a.m.–2:30 p.m.	Get up 6:30 a.m. Work 7:30 a.m.–2:30 p.m.	Get up 6:30 a.m. Work 7:30 a.m.–2:30 p.m.	Get up 6:30 a.m. Work 7:30 a.m.–2:30 p.m.	Get up 6:30 a.m. Work 7:30 a.m.–2:30 p.m.	Off
Afternoon	Visit parents	Yoga		Yoga			Do homework
Evening			Class 7:15–9:45 p.m.		Class 7:15–9:45 p.m.		
	Bed at 11:00 p.m.	Bed at 11:00 p.m.	Bed at 11:00 p.m.	Bed at 11:00 p.m.	Bed at 11:00 p.m.	Bed at 11:00 p.m.	

A Look at Allie's schedule on p. 94, and complete the sentences about it. Use the correct time expressions.

Time	**Part of Day / Day of Week**
at (time)	*in the* (morning / afternoon / evening)
from (time) *to* (time)	*on* (day of week)

Use *at* (time) and *from* (time / day) *to* (time / day) to indicate exact times and days.
Use *on* (day of week) or *in the* (morning / afternoon / evening) to indicate the day or part of day.

1. Allie goes to yoga _on Mondays and Wednesdays_ . (days)

2. She works _from Monday to Friday_ . (days)

3. She works _from 7:30 AM to 2:30 PM_ . (times)

4. She has classes _on Tuesdays and Thursdays_ . (days)

5. Her classes are _from 7:15 PM to 9:45 PM_ . (times)

6. Her days off are _on Saturdays and Sundays_ . (days)

7. She visits her parents _on Sundays_ . (day)

8. During the week, she usually goes to bed _at 11:00 PM_ and wakes up _at 6:30 AM._ . (times)

9. She does her homework _on Saturdays_ . (day)

B *Over to You* Think about your schedule. Complete the sentences below. Make them true for you.

1. I take classes (days) _on Mondays, Tuesdays, Wednesdays, and Thursdays_ .

2. My classes are (time) _from 9:00 AM to 3:00 PM_ .

3. I work (days) _on Wednesdays and Saturdays_ .

4. I work (time) _from 11:00 AM to 01:00 PM._ .

5. During the week, I go to sleep (time) _at 11:00 PM_ .

6. On the weekends, I go to sleep (time) _at 12:00 PM_ .

7. On Sundays, I get up (time) _at 08:00 AM._ .

8. I do my homework (time) _at 06:00 PM_ .

3 | Statements with Adverbs of Frequency

▶ Grammar Presentation

Adverbs of frequency describe how often something happens.	*Our neighbors **never drive** to work.* *They **always ride** their bikes.*

3.1 Adverbs of Frequency

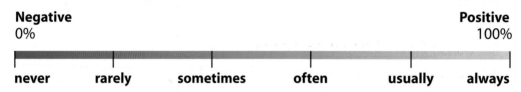

Negative
0%

Positive
100%

never   rarely   sometimes   often   usually   always

Rarely is not frequently used.

3.2 Adverbs of Frequency

Subject	Adverb of Frequency	Verb	
I You We They	**always** **usually** **often** **sometimes** **rarely** **never**	**work**	10 hours a day.
He She It		**works**	

Adverbs of Frequency with *Be*

Subject	*Be*	Adverb of Frequency	
I	**am**	**always** **usually** **often** **sometimes** **rarely** **never**	tired.
You We They	**are**		
He She It	**is**		

3.3 Using Adverbs of Frequency

a. Adverbs of frequency usually come after the verb *be*.	*I **am often** busy in the afternoon.* *She **is usually** tired in the morning.*
b. Adverbs of frequency usually come before other verbs.	*My parents **rarely eat** meat.* *Cristina **often rides** her bike to work.* *He **doesn't usually watch** TV.*
c. *Sometimes*, *usually*, and *often* can come before the verb OR at the beginning or end of a sentence.	*We **sometimes cook** for our family.* ***Sometimes** we **cook** for our family.* *We **cook** for our family **sometimes**.*
d. Do not begin or end sentences with *always* and *never*.	*Your grandparents are **always** active.* NOT ***Always** your grandparents are active.* NOT *Your grandparents are active **never**.*

▶ # Grammar Application

Exercise 3.1 Adverbs of Frequency with Simple Present

Unscramble the words to make sentences.

1. happy / My / always / is / brother / at work.

   My brother is always happy at work.

2. music. / He / listen to / does / not / often

   _____

3. slows down. / never / He

   _____

4. sometimes / He / seven / works / a week. / days

   _____

5. takes / He / a day off. / rarely

   _____

6. starts / in / work / He / at 3:00 / usually / the afternoon.

   _____

7. until 1:00 a.m. / doesn't / He / usually / finish

   _____

8. is / tired. / rarely / My brother

   _____

Exercise 3.2 More Adverbs of Frequency with Simple Present

A *Over to You* Read the sentences and check (✓) the boxes. Make them true for you.

Talk About Your Lifestyle

	never	sometimes	often	usually	always
1. I get eight hours of sleep at night.					
2. I fall asleep easily.					
3. I wake up at night.					
4. I exercise three times a week.					
5. I have dinner with friends on the weekend.					
6. I watch TV at night.					
7. I go to the library one day a month.					
8. I go away for vacation.					

B *Pair Work* Take turns saying your sentences from A with a partner.

A *I never get eight hours of sleep at night. How about you, Olga?*
B *I sometimes get eight hours of sleep at night.*

4 Avoid Common Mistakes ⚠

1. **For affirmative statements with *he/she/it*, use the base form of the verb + *-s / -es*.**

   relaxes
   He ~~relax~~ after lunch.

2. **For affirmative statements with *I/you/we/they* or a plural noun, use the base form of the verb.**

   go
   My parents ~~goes~~ out to dinner every Friday night.

3. **In negative statements, use *do not / don't* or *does not / doesn't* + the base form of the verb.**

   jog
   Maria does not ~~jogs~~ after dark.

4. **Do not use *do* or *does* in negative statements with *be*.**

   am not
   I ~~don't be~~ in an active social group.

5. **Do not use *be* with a simple present verb.**

   I ~~am~~ exercise on Tuesdays.

Editing Task Find and correct 10 more mistakes in the letter.

Dear Pedro,

    How are you? I'm fine. I'm in Vermont with my aunt and uncle. They ~~lives~~ *live* on a farm. The lifestyle here is very different. They are dairy farmers, so they are work hard every day. They usually get up at 4:30 a.m. They go to the barn and milk the cows. Cows makes a lot of noise in the
5 morning, so they usually wakes me up. Of course, I do not gets up until about 7:00 a.m. At 9:00, my uncle cook a wonderful breakfast. We all eat together. After that, he and I goes to the barn and works there. My aunt usually stay in the house. In the afternoon, there is more work. At night, I am
10 really tired, so I always goes to bed at 8:30! Usually my aunt and uncle don't be tired. They usually go to bed late!

    I hope your vacation is fun. See you soon!

Your friend,
15 Oscar

5 | Grammar for Writing ✏

Writing About Daily Life

Writers use the simple present with adverbs of frequency to write about routines and daily habits in people's lives.

Remember:

- **Use adverbs of frequency to show how often you do things.**

  I usually exercise in the mornings.   *Sometimes he goes for a run before breakfast.*

- **Use *never* or the negative simple present to show things you don't do. Don't use *never* and the negative simple present together.**

  They never work on the weekends.   *We do not stay up late during the week.*

Pre-writing Task

1 Read the paragraph below. When do the routines in the paragraph happen? How are the writer's routines and her husband's routines different?

Different Routines

My husband and I have very different routines. My husband usually goes to bed early. Sometimes he watches TV and then goes to bed around 9:00. I never go to bed early. I usually check my e-mail. I often surf the Internet. I never watch TV, but I sometimes read. Then, around midnight, I drink some warm milk and go to sleep. My husband always gets up early. He goes for a run, and then he makes coffee. When the coffee is ready, I get up.

2 Read the paragraph again. Underline the simple present verbs and circle the adverbs of frequency. Complete the chart.

The writer's routines	The writer's husband's routines
	goes to bed early

Writing Task

1 *Write* Use the paragraph in the Pre-writing Task to help you write about some of your routines, or compare your routines with the routines of another person. Think about your favorite time of day. What do you usually do or not do during this time? What does the other person usually do or not do?

Use sentences such as:

- I often _____ .
- She never _____ .
- We usually _____ .
- Sometimes I _____ .

2 *Self-Edit* Use the editing tips below to improve your sentences. Make any necessary changes.

1. Did you use the simple present and adverbs of frequency to write about daily life?
2. Did you use adverbs of frequency to show how often these daily routines happen?
3. Did you use *never* or *do not / does not* to show things that don't ever happen?
4. Did you avoid the mistakes in the Avoid Common Mistakes chart on page 99?

Simple Present *Yes / No* Questions and Short Answers

Daily Habits

1 Grammar in the Real World

A Do you get enough sleep? Do you have trouble sleeping? Read the news article below about sleeping habits. Answer the survey questions.

Do most people get enough sleep?

If you think "no," you are correct. The National Sleep Foundation's 2010 Sleep in America™ poll[1] shows that sleep is a problem for many people. About 75 percent agree that poor sleep can affect their work or family relationships. How are your sleep habits? To find out, answer the survey[2] questions below.

	Yes	No
1. **Do** you **fall asleep** in 30 minutes or less?	❑	❑
2. **Do** you **have** trouble falling asleep?	❑	❑
3. **Do** you **suffer** from insomnia?[3]	❑	❑
4. **Does** stress **keep** you awake?	❑	❑
5. **Do** you **take** any sleep medication?	❑	❑
6. **Do** you **wake up** during the night?	❑	❑
7. **Do** you **wake up** too early in the morning?	❑	❑
8. **Do** you **feel** very tired in the morning?	❑	❑
9. **Do** you **get** at least seven hours of sleep each night?	❑	❑
10. **Do** you **get** more sleep on the weekends?	❑	❑

[1]**poll:** a short questionnaire, usually one question | [2]**survey:** a set of questions to find out people's habits or beliefs about something | [3]**suffer from insomnia:** find it difficult to get to sleep or to sleep well

B *Comprehension Check* Circle the correct answer.

1. This article is about **health / sleep** habits.

2. Sleep is a **problem / hobby** for many people.

3. Many people believe poor sleep can affect their **work / friends**.

C *Notice* Find the questions in the news article, and choose the correct word to complete the questions. Then underline the subject of each sentence.

1. **Do / Does** most people get enough sleep?

2. **Do / Does** you suffer from insomnia?

3. **Do / Does** stress keep you awake?

Notice the use of *do* and *does*. Which word do you use for singular subjects? Which word do you use for plural subjects?

2 Simple Present *Yes / No* Questions and Short Answers

▶ Grammar Presentation

You can use simple present questions to ask about habits, routines, and facts.	**Do** you **wake up** early? **Does** she **suffer** from insomnia?

2.1 *Yes / No* Questions

Do / Does	Subject	Base Form of Verb	
Do	I you we they	**fall asleep**	in 30 minutes?
Does	he she it		

2.2 Short Answers

AFFIRMATIVE				NEGATIVE			
Yes	**Subject**	**Do/Does**		**No**	**Subject**	**Do/Does + Not**	
Yes,	I you we they	**do**.		No,	I you we they	**do not.** **don't.**	
	he she it	**does**.			he she it	**does not.** **doesn't.**	

2.3 Using Simple Present *Yes / No* Questions and Answers

a. For simple present *Yes / No* questions, use *Do* or *Does* with the base form of the verb.	***Do*** you **feel** tired every morning? ***Does*** he **wake up** during the night?
b. People usually use contractions in negative short answers.	"Do you watch TV all night?" "No, I **don't**."
Be careful! Negative full forms are very strong. You can sound angry.	"No, I **do not**!" (This can sound angry.)
c. You can give longer answers to *Yes / No* questions. It's friendly to give more information.	"Do you fall asleep easily?" "Yes, I usually fall asleep in about 15 minutes." "No, I often stay awake for an hour."
You can also give a short answer and then give more information in a separate sentence.	"Yes, I do. I usually fall asleep in about 15 minutes." "No, I don't. I often stay awake for an hour."
d. Some questions do not have a simple *yes* or *no* answer. You can answer *Well, . . .* and give a longer answer in speaking.	"Do you live with your family?" "**Well**, I live with my aunt and uncle."
Do not use *Well, . . .* to answer questions in academic writing, for example in compositions or tests.	"Does the average college student get a lot of sleep?" "The average student gets about six hours of sleep." NOT "~~Well~~, the average student gets about six hours of sleep."

▶ Grammar Application

Exercise 2.1 *Yes / No* Questions and Short Answers

A Complete the questions with *Do* or *Does*. Then write short answers. Make them true for you.

1. ___*Do*___ you get up early?   *Yes, I do./No, I don't.*
2. ___Does___ the sun wake you up?   Yes, it does.
3. ___Does___ your alarm clock play music?   Yes, it does
4. ___Do___ you often go back to sleep?   No, I don't
5. ___Do___ you like mornings?   No, I don't
6. ___Do___ you sleep until noon on the weekends?   No, I don't
7. ___Do___ you usually stay up past midnight?   Yes, I do
8. ___Do___ you study late at night?   No, I don't

B *Pair Work* Ask and answer the questions in A. Give short answers to your partner's questions.

A *Do you get up early?*

B *No, I don't.*

Exercise 2.2 More Yes / No Questions and Short Answers

A Complete the conversations about other habits. Write questions with the words in parentheses. Then complete the short answers.

Conversation 1

Lucy <u>*Do you and your brother share*</u> (you and your
(1)
brother/share) the cooking?

Malia No, <u>we don't</u> . I'm always busy with school.
(2)

Lucy So, <u>does your brother do</u> (your
(3)
brother/do) all the cooking?

Malia Yes, <u>he does</u> . He's a great cook.
(4)

Lucy <u>Does he work</u> (he/work)
(5)
in a restaurant?

Malia No, <u>he does not</u> .
(6)

Lucy Oh, <u>does he go</u> (he/go)
(7)
to cooking school?

Malia No, <u>he does not</u> . He just loves food.
(8)

Conversation 2

Lucy <u>Do your grandparents live</u> (your grandparents/live) nearby?
(1)

Malia Yes, <u>they do</u> . They live next door.
(2)

Lucy Nice. <u>Do you and your family see</u> (you and your family/see) them often?
(3)

Malia No, <u>we do not</u> . They're at the hospital a lot.
(4)

Lucy Oh, I'm sorry. <u>Do they need</u> (they/need) help?
(5)

Malia No, <u>they do not</u> . They're fine. They work there. They volunteer at the hospital.
(6)

Lucy Oh? <u>Do they visit</u> (they/visit) patients and help the nurses?
(7)

Malia No, <u>they do not</u> . They both work in the hospital gift shop.
(8)

B *Pair Work* Practice the conversations in A with a partner.

Exercise 2.3 ◀)) Pronunciation Focus: *Do you . . . ?*

In speaking, people often say *Do you* very fast.
It can sound like one word ("D'you").
Always write *Do you* as two words, but say it fast so it sounds like one word ("D'you").

A ◀)) Listen to the questions about people's music habits. Repeat the questions. Say *Do you* fast, as one word.

Do you fall asleep with music on?

Do you like loud music?

Do you dance when you listen to music?

Do you listen to music all the time?

Do you study with music on?

Do you sing along to music?

Do you have an MP3 player?

B *Pair Work* Ask and answer the questions in A. Give a short answer first, and then give more information in a second sentence. Use *Well, . . .* for some answers.

A *Do you like loud music?*
B *No, I don't. I prefer soft music.*

A *Do you listen to music all the time?*
B *Well, I don't listen to music when I'm in class.*

Exercise 2.4 Yes / No Questions in a Survey

A *Over to You* Write questions for these habits. Then ask your classmates these questions. Write their names in the chart.

Who . . . ?		Name
falls asleep with the TV on	1. *Do you fall asleep with the TV on?*	
falls asleep to music	2. _____	
talks in his or her sleep	3. _____	
dreams a lot	4. _____	
remembers his or her dreams	5. _____	
walks in his or her sleep	6. _____	
hits the "snooze" button[1] 2 or 3 times	7. _____	
gets enough sleep	8. _____	

[1]**snooze button:** a button on an alarm clock that stops the alarm for a short time and makes the alarm ring again in a few minutes

B *Pair Work* Tell a partner about four classmates and their sleeping habits.

Delia talks in her sleep.

3 | Avoid Common Mistakes ⚠

1. **Use *Do* with plural subjects and with *you*.**
   Do
   ~~Does~~ your roommates stay up late?

2. **Use *Does* with singular subjects (except *you*).**
   Does
   ~~Do~~ this alarm clock work?

3. **Use *Do / Does* in simple present questions with *have*.**
   Do you have
   ~~Have you~~ an MP3 player?

4. **Do not use *Do / Does* in questions with *be*.**
   Is
   ~~Do~~ your cell phone new?

5. **Do not use *Be* with other simple present verbs.**
   Do
   ~~Are~~ you agree?

Editing Task

Find and correct seven more mistakes in these questions about sleeping habits.

1. ~~Have you~~ *Do you have* trouble falling asleep?
2. ~~Are~~ *Do* you sleep on your stomach, your back, or your side?
3. ~~Have you~~ *Do you have* a TV in your bedroom?
4. ~~Does~~ *Do* you dream in color or in black-and-white?
5. ~~Do~~ *Does* a dream ever scare you?   *adverb nuance (verb)   A dream does scare me.*
6. ~~Does~~ *Do* loud noises wake you up at night?
7. ~~Do~~ *Are* you a light sleeper or a deep sleeper?
8. ~~Does~~ *Do* you fall asleep quickly?

4 | Grammar for Writing ✎

Writing Survey Questions About Habits and Routines

Writers use simple present *Yes/No* questions in surveys to find out about people's daily habits and routines.

Remember:

- **Start your questions with *Do* and *Does*.**
  <u>Do</u> you eat breakfast before work?   <u>Does</u> your workplace have coffee?

- **You can use *ever* or *usually* in your questions to find out how often things happen.**
  Do you <u>ever</u> work at night?   Does your homework <u>usually</u> take an hour or more?

Pre-writing Task

1 *Pair Work* Read the paragraphs below and the survey questions that a student wrote about living with others. Ask and answer the questions with a partner. Take turns.

Habits at Home

Most people do not live alone. They live with their parents, their families, or friends. There are many wonderful things about living with other people. For example, there is always somebody that you can talk to when you feel sad or angry. The house can be a comfortable place. However, sometimes there are problems when many people live

5 together. For example, people argue a lot, or the house is very noisy all the time. Good communication is important. Everyone can talk to each other and solve problems. Here are some questions about living situations. Please answer the questions. What is your living situation like? Is your living situation a good one?

    1. Do the <u>people</u> in your home help with the housework and chores?

10   2. Do the people in your home (usually) help each other when there are problems?

    3. Do you ever spend time together and talk about your lives?

    4. Do the people in your home usually enjoy each other's company?

    5. Does everyone eat meals together?

    6. Do you think that you have a good living situation?

15   The answers to these questions are important. I believe that people who answer *yes* to these questions have good living situations.

2 Read the paragraphs and the questions again. Underline the subject and *do* or *does* in the questions. Circle *ever* and *usually*.

Writing Task

1 *Write* Write a short paragraph and some survey questions about people's habits or things they do every day. Use the paragraphs and survey in the Pre-writing Task to help you. Choose one topic below:

- food-shopping routines
- homework or study habits
- morning or evening routines
- getting to work or school
- mealtime routines
- your own idea

Think about what you know about the topic and what you want to find out. At the end, give your survey to your classmates. Write about what you find out.

2 *Self-Edit* Use the editing tips below to improve your sentences. Make any necessary changes.

1. Did you use the simple present to talk about a topic and write survey questions about that topic?
2. Did you use *Do* and *Does* correctly?
3. Did you use *ever* or *usually* in some of your questions?
4. Did you avoid the mistakes in the Avoid Common Mistakes chart on page 107?

UNIT 10

Simple Present Information Questions

Cultural Holidays

1 Grammar in the Real World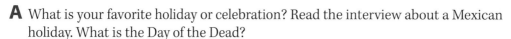

A What is your favorite holiday or celebration? Read the interview about a Mexican holiday. What is the Day of the Dead?

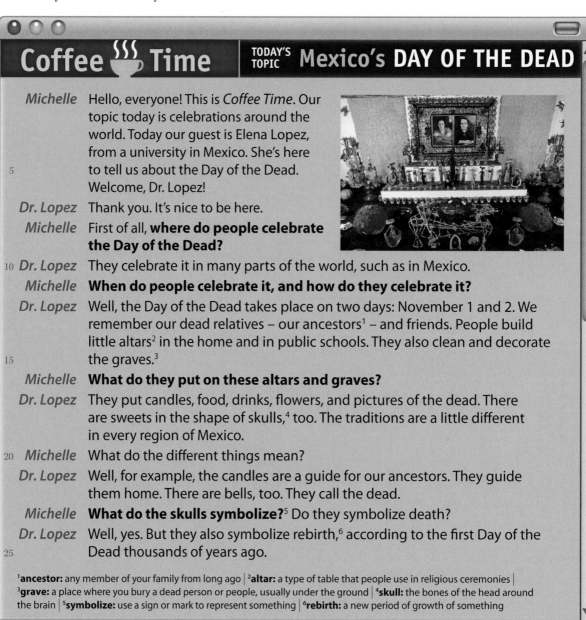

Coffee Time — TODAY'S TOPIC **Mexico's DAY OF THE DEAD**

Michelle Hello, everyone! This is *Coffee Time*. Our topic today is celebrations around the world. Today our guest is Elena Lopez, from a university in Mexico. She's here
5   to tell us about the Day of the Dead. Welcome, Dr. Lopez!

Dr. Lopez Thank you. It's nice to be here.

Michelle First of all, **where do people celebrate the Day of the Dead?**

10 **Dr. Lopez** They celebrate it in many parts of the world, such as in Mexico.

Michelle **When do people celebrate it, and how do they celebrate it?**

Dr. Lopez Well, the Day of the Dead takes place on two days: November 1 and 2. We remember our dead relatives – our ancestors[1] – and friends. People build little altars[2] in the home and in public schools. They also clean and decorate
15   the graves.[3]

Michelle **What do they put on these altars and graves?**

Dr. Lopez They put candles, food, drinks, flowers, and pictures of the dead. There are sweets in the shape of skulls,[4] too. The traditions are a little different in every region of Mexico.

20 **Michelle** What do the different things mean?

Dr. Lopez Well, for example, the candles are a guide for our ancestors. They guide them home. There are bells, too. They call the dead.

Michelle **What do the skulls symbolize?[5]** Do they symbolize death?

Dr. Lopez Well, yes. But they also symbolize rebirth,[6] according to the first Day of the
25   Dead thousands of years ago.

[1]**ancestor:** any member of your family from long ago | [2]**altar:** a type of table that people use in religious ceremonies | [3]**grave:** a place where you bury a dead person or people, usually under the ground | [4]**skull:** the bones of the head around the brain | [5]**symbolize:** use a sign or mark to represent something | [6]**rebirth:** a new period of growth of something

B *Comprehension Check* Choose the correct answers.

1. On the Day of the Dead, people remember _____.
   a. their parents   b. their dead relatives   c. their children

2. People put pictures of the dead _____.
   a. on altars   b. on sweets   c. on skulls

3. The Day of the Dead takes place _____.
   a. every month   b. one day a year   c. on November 1 and 2

4. People _____ their ancestors' graves.
   a. decorate   b. paint   c. celebrate

C *Notice* Answer the questions with the correct question word. Use the interview to help you.

1. Which word asks a question about **time**?   What   When   Where
2. Which word asks a question about **places**?   What   When   Where
3. Which word asks a question about **things**?   What   When   Where

What word comes after *when*, *where*, and *what*?

2 | Simple Present Information Questions — Wh-questions

▶ Grammar Presentation

Information questions begin with a *Wh-* word (*Who, What, When, Where, Why,* or *How*). They ask for information and cannot be answered with a simple *yes* or *no*.	***Where** do people celebrate the Day of the Dead?* ***When** do Americans celebrate Independence Day?*

2.1 Information Questions

Wh- word	Do / Does	Subject	Base Form of Verb	
Who		I you we they	**see**	at school?
What	**do**		**eat**	at parties?
When			**celebrate**	that holiday?
What time			**begin**	the celebration?
Where		he she it	**study**	for school?
Why	**does**		**live**	at home?
How			**meet**	new people?

2.2 Using Simple Present Information Questions

a. Use a *Wh-* word with *do* before *I, you, we, they,* and plural nouns.	***When do*** *you celebrate the holiday?*
Use a *Wh-* word with *does* before *he, she, it,* and singular nouns.	***Why does*** *she study Spanish?*
b. Use simple present information questions to ask for specific information.	*"**Where** do you live?"* *"I live in Mexico City."* *"**What time** do you start work?"* *"8:30."*
c. Use simple present information questions to ask about habits, facts, traditions, and regular activities.	*"**When** do they celebrate the Day of the Dead?"* *"In November."* *"**Why** does she travel to Mexico every year?"* *"Because she has family there."*
d. You can answer information questions with a short or long answer.	*"**What** do you eat on Thanksgiving?"* Short answer: *"Turkey and pie."* Long answer: *"I eat turkey and pie."*

2.3 Using *Wh-* Words

a. Use *Who* to ask about people.	*"**Who** do you remember on the Day of the Dead?"* *"I remember my grandmother."*
b. Use *What* to ask about things.	*"**What** do you study?"* *"Spanish and history."*
c. Use *When* to ask about time (days, months, years, seasons, parts of the day).	*"**When** do you celebrate Chinese New Year?"* *"In January or February."*
d. Use *What time* to ask about clock time.	*"**What time** does your class finish?"* *"4:30. / Five o'clock."*
e. Use *Where* to ask about places.	*"**Where** does she work?"* *"At the University of Mexico."*
f. Use *Why* to ask about reasons.	*"**Why** do you like celebrations?"* *"Because they're always fun."*
g. Use *How* to ask about manner – the way people do something.	*"**How** do you celebrate your birthday?"* *"We eat at my favorite restaurant."*

▶ Grammar Application

Exercise 2.1 Questions with *Who, What, When, Where, How*

A Complete the questions with *Who, What, When, Where,* or *How* and *do* or *does.*

1. **A** <u>*Where*</u> <u>*do*</u> people celebrate the Day of the Dead? **B** In Mexico.

2. **A** _____ _____ they celebrate the Day of the Dead? **B** On November 1 and 2.

3. **A** _____ _____ they remember? **B** Their dead relatives and friends.

4. **A** _____ _____ they decorate? **B** Graves and altars.

5. **A** _____ _____ they put pictures of the dead? **B** On altars.

6. **A** _____ _____ they decorate the graves? **B** With flowers, candles, food, and drinks.

B *Over to You* Unscramble the words and add *do* or *does* to make questions. Then write answers that are true for you.

1. what celebration / you / like / the best / ?

   A <u>*What celebration do you like the best?*</u>

   B _____

2. when / you / celebrate / it / ?

   A _____

   B _____

3. who / you / celebrate / it / with / ?

   A _____

   B _____

4. what / you / usually / do / ?

   A _____

   B _____

5. where / you / celebrate / it / ?

A _____

B _____

6. what / you / usually / eat / ?

A _____

B _____

7. when / it / usually / end / ?

A _____

B _____

C *Pair Work* Ask and answer the questions in B with a partner.

Exercise 2.2 Questions with *When* and *What Time*

A Complete the questions with *When* or *What time* and *do* or *does*.

1. *A* _*When*_ _*do*_ you graduate?   *B* On June 15.

2. *A* _____ _____ you have the ceremony?   *B* At 3:30.

3. *A* _____ _____ Sandi turn 21?   *B* Next Saturday.

4. *A* _____ _____ her birthday party start?   *B* At 7:00.

5. *A* _____ _____ you celebrate Thanksgiving in the   *B* At the end of November.
   United States?

6. *A* _____ _____ your family usually have the meal?   *B* In the late afternoon.

7. *A* _____ _____ you usually start cooking on that day? *B* At about 8:00 a.m.

B *Pair Work* Ask and answer the questions in A with a partner.

Exercise 2.3 Asking Information Questions

A Read the paragraph about a holiday celebration in Massachusetts. Write information questions using the words in parentheses. Find the verbs in the paragraph, and use the information to write your questions. Remember to use *do* and *does* in your questions.

One of my favorite holidays is Patriots' Day in the Boston, Massachusetts, area. Every year, Boston residents celebrate Patriots' Day on the third Monday of April. On this day, people remember the beginning of the American Revolutionary War. Many towns have parades and speeches.[1] The second important event is the Boston Marathon.[2] The marathon happens every year on Patriots' Day. The race starts around 10:00 a.m. in Hopkinton and ends in Boston. Thousands of people watch runners from all over the world. The third event is the special Patriots' Day baseball game. The Boston Red Sox play a team from another town. The game starts around 11:00 a.m. in Boston.

[1]**speech:** a formal talk | [2]**marathon:** a race in which people run 26 miles and 385 yards (42.195 kilometers)

1. (what / people / celebrate) *What do people celebrate on the third Monday of April?*
2. (what / people / remember) _____
3. (what / towns / have) _____
4. (when / marathon / happen) _____
5. (what time / marathon / start) _____
6. (where / marathon / start) _____
7. (who / people / watch) _____

B ***Pair Work*** Ask and answer the questions in A with a partner.

A What do people celebrate on the third Monday of April?
B They celebrate Patriots' Day.

Exercise 2.4 🔊 Pronunciation Focus: Intonation in Questions

In information questions, our voice usually *goes down*. We call this falling intonation.	Where do you go on va**ca**tion? Why do you stay **home**? When do you see your **re**latives?
In *Yes / No* questions, our voice often *goes up*. We call this rising intonation.	Do you celebrate Me**mo**rial Day? Is that your favorite day of the **year**? Does she work at **night**?

A 🔊 Listen to the questions and answers. Mark the questions with ➚ for rising intonation and ➘ for falling intonation.

1. *A* Excuse me. Are you from Japan? ➚

   B Yes, I am. I'm from Tokyo.

2. *A* Can I ask you some questions? _____

   B Sure!

3. *A* What's your favorite holiday in Japan? _____

   B New Year's Day.

4. *A* Why is it your favorite? _____

   B Because we have special food for the holiday, and we relax all day.

5. *A* Do you help your mother with the cooking? _____

   B Yes, I do. We also see all our relatives on New Year's Day.

6. *A* Do you play any special games? _____

   B No, not really. But we watch some special TV programs.

7. *A* What else do you do on New Year's Day? _____

   B Well, we read all our holiday cards then.

8. *A* Do you really save all the cards to open on the same day? _____

   B Yes, it's a special custom.

B 🔊 Listen and repeat the questions.

5 | Grammar for Writing ✎

Using Questions to Write About Special Days

Writers use information questions in the simple present to help them think of ideas about a topic. They use the answers to help them write their paragraphs.

Remember:

- **Start your questions with *Who, What, When, Where, What time, Why,* or *How*.**

  What do you do on your birthday?   *When do you eat your Thanksgiving meal?*

- **Use *How often* to find out specific information about how frequently people do things.**

  How often does your daughter visit for Mother's Day?

Pre-writing Task

1 Read the student's paragraph below. Have you ever celebrated Mardi Gras?

Mardi Gras

what

Mardi Gras is a popular celebration. It takes place once a year for several days in February or March. Many people celebrate it around the world. The celebrations are all different. For example, in the United States, New Orleans is famous for its Mardi Gras celebrations. During Mardi Gras, people wear colorful costumes and march in parades. Some parades are at night. Marchers throw colorful necklaces to the people watching the parades. The beads are very popular. There is a lot of jazz music and dancing. People love Mardi Gras because it is a good time to relax and enjoy life.

2 Read the paragraph again. Notice how the sentences answer information questions about Mardi Gras. Find a sentence that gives an answer for each of these *wh-* words: *What, When, Who,* and *Why*. Write the correct *wh-* word above the sentences you find.

Writing Task

1 *Write* Use the paragraph in the Pre-writing Task to help you write about a special day in your life. Make a list of information questions about your special day. Use the answers as you write.

2 *Self-Edit* Use the editing tips below to improve your sentences. Make any necessary changes.

1. Did you use information questions about your special day to help you think of ideas?
2. Did you use the answers from the questions to help you write your paragraph?
3. Did you use *Wh-* words and *do / does* in your questions?
4. Did you avoid the mistakes in the Avoid Common Mistakes chart on page 120?

Grammar for Writing

Using Questions to Write About Special Days

UNIT 11

Conjunctions: *And, But, Or*; *Because*

Time Management

1 Grammar in the Real World

A Do you have enough time for school, work, and family? Read the article below. What is one way to manage your time well?

Time for Everything

Many adults say they want more time. They are busy with work, family, **and** school, **and** they often don't get everything
5 done. People feel stressed **because** there is not enough time to do it all. However, there are some simple ways to manage your time well **and** avoid stress.

One way is to identify the important **or**
10 necessary tasks for that day. Then create a schedule **or** a "to do" list.[1] When you finish your important tasks, you can move on to the next, less important ones. Soon your tasks are done, **and** there is hopefully some
15 extra time for fun activities.

Another way is to do important tasks on the same days every week. For example, you can do your laundry every Monday, **and**
20 go to the gym on Tuesday and Thursday mornings before work or school. Always do the tasks on the same days. That way, you can plan around these important tasks **and** have time for other things. Some people don't like schedules, lists,
25 or weekly plans. Instead, they use the notes or calendar features on their cell phones. Put a reminder[2] for the task on your phone, **but** don't forget to do it!

These ideas can help you improve your
30 time management.[3] When you make plans and complete them, you feel good **and** can do more.

To Do:

grocery shopping

laundry

walk the dog

Monday	Tuesday
7:00 laundry	8:00 gym
9:00 work	10:00 class

[1]**"to do" list:** a list of things you need to do | [2]**reminder:** something that helps someone remember, like an alarm on a phone |
[3]**time management:** being in control of your time; planning and using your time well

B *Comprehension Check* Answer the questions. Use the article to help you.

1. What do most adults not have enough of?
2. What are two ways to manage your time?
3. What happens when people make plans and complete them?

C *Notice* Find the words *and*, *but*, *or*, and *because* in the article. Then complete the sentences.

1. They are busy with work, family, _____ school.

2. People feel stressed _____ there is not enough time to do it all.

3. Some people don't like schedules, lists, _____ weekly plans.

4. Put a reminder for the task on your phone, _____ don't forget to do it!

2 | *And, But, Or*

▶ Grammar Presentation

And, but, and *or* are coordinating conjunctions. They connect words, phrases, and clauses.	People are busy with family **and** work. I like to exercise, **but** I don't have time for it every day. She studies in the morning **or** after work.

2.1 *And, But, Or* for Connecting Words and Phrases

Connecting Words	*Time **and** money* are valuable. She sleeps only **five or six** hours a night.
Connecting Phrases	I always **make a schedule and look at it often**. I have "to do" lists **on my computer but not on my phone**. Do you work **during the day or at night**?

2.2 *And, But, Or* for Connecting Clauses

First Clause		Second Clause
You have more time in your day,	**and**	you feel less stressed.
Some people use their time well,	**but**	other people do not.
You can make a list,	**or**	you can schedule tasks on the same days.

2.3 Using *And, But, Or*

a. Use *and*, *but*, and *or* to connect words, phrases, and clauses.	Time **and** money are valuable. He has time **but** not money. Do you use schedules, **or** do you make "to do" lists?
b. Use *and* to join two or more ideas.	Maria makes time for school, family, **and** work. I study **and** work every day. I make a "to do" list, **and** I check the list often during the day.
c. Use *but* to show contrast or surprising information.	José works hard, **but** he also has fun. He always makes a schedule, **but** he rarely follows it.
d. Use *or* to show a choice of two alternatives.	You can make lists **or** schedules. I exercise **or** do laundry after I study. Is he at school **or** at work?
e. Use a comma when *and*, *but*, and *or* connect two clauses.	My family gets together at night, **and** we talk about our day. Sonya wakes up early, **but** she is always late for work.

▶ # Grammar Application

Exercise 2.1 Choosing *And, But, Or*

A Read the sentences about two types of people. Complete the sentences with *and*, *but*, or *or*. Add commas where necessary.

The Organized Person

1. Every day I wake up*, and* I make a long "to do" list.

2. I usually use the "notes" feature on my phone for important tasks _____ I always do them.

3. I don't like to forget appointments _____ be late.

4. I like to be busy _____ I feel good when I get things done.

The Disorganized Person

5. Sometimes I make lists _____ I usually lose them.

6. I have a lot of appointments _____ a lot of things to do every day.

7. I try to be on time _____ I am often late for appointments.

8. I am always busy _____ I don't get things done.

B *Over to You* Read the sentences in A with a partner. Which statements are true for you? Tell your partner.

Exercise 2.2 Punctuating Sentences with *And, But, Or*

A Correct the sentences below about ways to add time to a busy day. Add capital letters, periods, and commas as necessary.

1. a. Jane wants to read more but she doesn't have the time

   Jane wants to read more, but she doesn't have the time.

   b. now she listens to audiobooks in the car and during her breaks at work

   _____

   c. she listens to a book or a podcast every day and feels good about herself

   _____

2. a. James is very busy and often doesn't do his homework or study

   _____

   b. he worries about his grades and gets very upset

   _____

   c. finally, he talks about his problem with a classmate and they decide to help each other

   _____

   d. he and his classmate now talk on the phone every day and work on their homework together

   _____

B *Group Work* Make a list of four study tips. Use *and*, *but*, and *or* in your sentences.

Exercise 2.3 More *And, But, Or*

Good time management includes time for fun activities. Complete the sentences with your ideas about things you do for fun. Use *and*, *but*, or *or*.

1. On the weekends, I _watch TV and garden_____ .

2. Once a day, I _____ .

3. In the evenings, I _____ .

4. Sometimes I _____ .

Exercise 2.4 Vocabulary Focus: Expressions with *And* and *Or*

Data from the Real World		
English has many expressions using *and* and *or*. The nouns usually occur in the order they appear below.	*Do you like peanut butter and jelly?* NOT *Do you like jelly and peanut butter?*	
Common "noun *and* noun" expressions for food	cream **and** sugar salt **and** pepper bread **and** butter	peanut butter **and** jelly fish **and** chips
Common "noun *and* noun" expressions for relationships	mom **and** dad brother **and** sister husband **and** wife	Mr. **and** Mrs. father **and** son mother **and** daughter
Other common "noun *and* noun" expressions	night **and** day men **and** women name **and** address	ladies **and** gentlemen boys **and** girls
Common expressions with *or*	cash **or** credit	coffee **or** tea
Common "adjective *and* adjective" expressions	black **and** white old **and** new	nice **and** warm

A Complete the questions.

1. Do you like _cream_ and sugar with your coffee?

2. Do your _____ and dad live in the United States?

3. Do you have brothers and _____ ?

4. Do you work _____ and day?

5. Do you like black and _____ movies?

6. Do you think _____ and women have really different interests?

7. Do you put salt and _____ on your food?

8. Do you usually pay with _____ or credit?

9. Do you ever eat peanut butter and _____ sandwiches?

10. Do you prefer _____ or tea?

B *Pair Work* Take turns asking and answering the questions in A with a partner. Use complete sentences in your answers.

> A *Do you like cream and sugar with your coffee?*
> B *I like sugar, but I don't like cream.*

3 | *Because*

▶ Grammar Presentation

Because introduces the reason for or cause of something.	EFFECT CAUSE *People feel stressed **because** there is not enough time.*

3.1 *Because* for Connecting Clauses

a. *Because* shows a cause-and-effect relationship.	EFFECT CAUSE *I am always late **because** I don't like to get up early.*
Clauses with *because* must have a subject and a verb.	SUBJECT VERB *Some people send e-mail reminders **because they** **want** to remember their tasks.*
b. A clause with *because* is <u>not</u> a complete sentence. It needs the main clause to form a complete sentence.	MAIN CLAUSE *I am always late **because** I don't like to get up early.* NOT *I am always late.* ***Because** I don't like to get up early.*
c. *Because* can come before or after the main clause. Use a comma when *because* comes first in a sentence.	MAIN CLAUSE ***Because** I don't like to get up early*, *I am always late.* MAIN CLAUSE *I am always late **because** I don't like to get up early.*
d. In speaking, you can answer a question starting with *because*. Do not do this in writing.	*Why are you at school?* Say: ***Because** I want to learn English.*

▶ Grammar Application

Exercise 3.1 Cause-and-Effect Relationships with *Because*

Match the effect on the left with the cause on the right.

1. John is tired __*c*__   a. because his foot hurts.

2. Tanya is usually late _____   b. because he never eats breakfast.

3. Dan is often hungry _____   c̸. because he doesn't sleep enough.

4. Eric walks slowly _____   d. because he works during the day.

5. Sue takes her brother to   e. because she doesn't put reminders on
    school _____   her phone.

6. Maya and Sara sleep late _____   f. because their mother doesn't have time.

7. Jack takes classes at night _____ g. because their alarm clocks don't work.

Exercise 3.2 ◄)) The Position of *Because*

Put *because* in the correct place in each sentence. Add commas where necessary. Then listen and compare your answers.

Bob, Jamal, Tony, and Leo are roommates. They study at the local community college. Each roommate has a problem with time.

1. Leo works at night *because* he goes to school during the day.

2. Tony can only study in the mornings he thinks more clearly then.

3. Bob's alarm clock doesn't work he is always late.

4. Jamal can't study at home his roommates are too noisy.

5. Leo forgets to write his assignments down he often misses them.

6. Tony and Jamal sometimes miss class they play basketball instead.

Exercise 3.3 Combining Sentences with *Because*

Label each clause with *C* for "cause" and *E* for "effect." Then combine the sentences with *because*. Do not change the order of the clauses.

1. __E__ Brendon does well in class. __C__ He studies every day.

   Brendon does well in class because he studies every day.

2. __C__ Tanya's alarm clock does not work. __E__ She is often late for work.

   Because Tanya's alarm clock does not work, she is often late for work.

3. _____ Alan has three reminders about _____ He doesn't want to forget about it.
   the meeting on his phone.

   _____

4. _____ Wanda is always hungry at work. _____ She doesn't have time for lunch.

   _____

5. _____ Karin starts work very early. _____ She drinks a lot of coffee.

   _____

6. _____ Blanca works during the day. _____ She takes night classes.

   _____

7. _____ Jared keeps a "to do" list. _____ He has a lot of work.

   _____

Exercise 3.4 Giving Reasons with *Because*

Complete the sentences. Make them true for you.

1. I take English classes because _____.

2. I wake up at _____ because _____.
   (time)

3. I live in _____ because _____.
   (town/city)

4. I like _____ because _____.
   (class)

5. I go to bed at _____ because _____.
   (time)

4 Avoid Common Mistakes ⚠️

1. **Do not use a comma when you join two words or two phrases.**
   Lisa creates a schedule ̸and a list every day.

2. **Use a comma when you join two clauses with *and*, *but*, and *or*.**
   I need to study for the test ̭and then I have to work!

3. **Use *and to* add information. Use *but* to show a contrast. Use *or* to show a choice.**
   Sam is always late, ~~and~~ he gets his work done.   but

4. **Do not use a comma if *because* is in the second part of the sentence.**
   Jake is always on time ̸because he takes the 8:00 bus to school every day.

   But do use a comma if *because* is in the first part of the sentence.
   Because Lily makes a daily schedule ̭she never forgets to do her tasks.

5. **Use *because* to state the reason (cause) for something. The other part of the sentence states the result (effect).**
   Because Kylie writes her assignments on her calendar,
   ~~Kylie writes her assignments on her calendar because~~ she doesn't forget them.
   Kylie doesn't forget her assignments because
   ~~Because Kylie doesn't forget her assignments,~~ she writes them on her calendar.

Editing Task

Read the story about Professor Kwan's class on time management. Find and correct
9 more mistakes.

A Useful Class

Every year, Professor Kwan teaches a class on time management. Many students
like to take her class. Sometimes the class fills up quickly ̸because it is so popular.
Students know that they need to register early – in person and online. This is the first
lesson of the time-management class.

5   In this class, Professor Kwan talks about different ways for students to organize
their time. Her students often complain about the stress they have but how little

time they have. Professor Kwan always tells her students to buy a calendar. She says students can use an electronic calendar but a paper calendar. Because her students get organized they use their calendar every day. She tells students to find time to study

10 at least once a day – either after school and at night. When students plan their time well, they feel in control and confident.

This is not the only thing that Professor Kwan teaches in the class. Students have a lot of stress because it is also important to find time to relax, and exercise. Professor Kwan's class is so popular, because all students need help with time management. At the

15 end of her class, students have less stress and they have great time-management skills!

5 | Grammar for Writing ✎

Describing the Way You Do Something

Writers use *and*, *but*, *or*, and *because* to combine ideas and to show relationships between ideas. They can use these conjunctions to write about something they do regularly. Remember:

- **Use *and*, *but*, or *or* to combine words, phrases, or clauses.**
  I usually do my homework on the bus <u>and</u> on my lunch break.
  She does her homework at night, <u>but</u> sometimes she falls asleep.
  His homework is never late <u>or</u> incomplete.

- **Use *because* to show a cause-and-effect relationship between two sentences.**
  She has very little time <u>because</u> she has two jobs.

Pre-writing Task

1 Read the paragraph below. When and where does the writer do her homework? Why?

Doing My Homework

I'm always busy (because) I work and I take classes. I don't have a lot of time for homework because of this. Because my homework is important, I do it in the library before or after my class. The library opens at 7:00 a.m.,
5 and my class starts at 8:00 a.m. The library is quiet at 7:00 a.m. because it is often empty then. Sometimes I ask the librarians for help. They are usually very nice and helpful, but sometimes they are busy with their work. After class, the library is full, but it is still a good place
10 to study.

2 Read the paragraph again. Circle the conjunctions *and*, *but*, *or*, and *because*. Which conjunctions connect words? Which connect phrases? Which connect clauses?

Writing Task

1 *Write*   Use the paragraph in the Pre-writing Task to help you write about something you need to do regularly. Do you schedule time for this activity? When and where do you do this activity? Explain why. Write about how you:

- clean house
- do dishes
- do homework
- do laundry
- exercise
- go food shopping
- make meals
- pay bills
- take care of children

Use *and*, *but*, *or*, and *because* to combine ideas and show relationships between ideas.

2 *Self-Edit*   Use the editing tips below to improve your sentences. Make any necessary changes.

1. Did you use conjunctions to write about something you do regularly?
2. Did you use *and*, *but*, and *or* to connect words, phrases, or clauses?
3. Did you use *because* to show cause-and-effect relationships?
4. Did you avoid the mistakes in the Avoid Common Mistakes chart on page 130?

Simple Past Statements

Success Stories

1 | Grammar in the Real World

A Do you know people who don't give up easily? Read the article below. What do you learn about this band?

A Band That Didn't Give Up[1]

Writers, artists, singers, and inventors[2] often feel discouraged[3] when others tell them they are not good enough. Some people give up. Others, like a group of young musicians in the 1960s,
5 don't let it stop them.

In December 1961, a record company executive[4] **traveled** to Liverpool, England. He **went** to listen to a new rock 'n' roll band. The executive **thought** the band **had** talent and
10 **invited** them to an audition[5] in London. The group **went** to London and **played** on New Year's Day 1962. After the audition, they **went** home and **waited** for a phone call. They **didn't hear** any news for weeks.

15 Finally, the company executive **told** the band manager, "Guitar groups are on the way out,[6] Mr. Epstein." So the record company **didn't give** the band a contract.[7]

But the band **didn't give up**. In the end, they **signed** a contract with another company and **became** a very famous band: The Beatles.

[1]**give up:** stop trying | [2]**inventor:** someone who designs or create new things | [3]**discouraged:** not confident to try again | [4]**executive:** person in a high position in a company who manages and makes decisions | [5]**audition:** short performance given to show ability | [6]**out:** not fashionable; not popular | [7]**contract:** written legal agreement

B *Comprehension Check* Are these sentences true or false? Use the article to help you. Correct the false sentences.

1. The executive traveled to London in December 1961.   True   False
2. The executive invited the band to London.   True   False
3. The band went to London and played on New Year's Eve.   True   False
4. The company didn't call the band immediately.   True   False
5. The band signed a contract with another company.   True   False

C *Notice* Answer the questions. Use the article to help you.

1. Can you find the past forms of these verbs in the article?

Present	travel	invite	play	wait	sign
Simple Past	traveled	invited	played	waited	signed

2. What do the simple past verbs in question 1 have in common?

3. Can you find the past forms of these verbs in the article?

Base Form	go	think	have	tell	become
Simple Past	went	thought	had	told	became

4. How are these simple past verbs different from the verbs in question 1?

2 | Simple Past Statements: Regular Verbs

▶ Grammar Presentation

The simple past describes events that started and ended before now.	In 1961, he **traveled** to Liverpool. The band **played** for two hours. They **didn't hear** any news for weeks.

2.1 Affirmative Statements

Subject	Simple Past Verb	
I You We They He / She / It	**started**	in 1962.

2.2 Negative Statements

Subject	*Did + Not*	Base Form of Verb	
I You We They He / She / It	**did not** **didn't**	**sign**	a contract.

2.3 Using Simple Past Statements

a. Use the simple past for events that started and ended in the past.

```
●————————————————————————————————
the past                                              now
```

It can be one event or repeated events.

*He **traveled** to Liverpool.*
*The band **played** in clubs every week.*
*They **didn't hear** any news.*

b. You can use the simple past to describe a feeling in the past.

*He **didn't like** the band.*

2.4 Spelling: Regular Simple Past Verbs

a. For most verbs, add -*ed*.

work → work**ed**

b. For verbs ending in *e*, add -*d*.

live → liv**ed**

c. For verbs ending in consonant + *y*, change *y* to *i* and add -*ed*.

study → stud**ied**

d. For verbs ending in vowel + *y*, add -*ed*.

play → play**ed**

e. For one-syllable verbs ending in consonant-vowel-consonant, double the consonant.

plan → pla**nned**

f. Do not double the consonant if the verb ends in -*x* or -*w*.

show → show**ed**

g. For two-syllable verbs ending in consonant-vowel-consonant and stressed on the first syllable, do not double the consonant.

travel → trave**led**

h. For two-syllable verbs ending in consonant-vowel-consonant and stressed on the second syllable, double the consonant.

control → contro**lled**

Here are some of the most common regular simple past verbs.

called	wanted	started	happened
worked	lived	tried	moved
looked	talked	liked	decided

▶ Spelling and Pronunciation Rules for Regular Verbs in Simple Past: See page A21.
▶ Common Regular and Irregular Verbs: See page A15.

▶ Grammar Application

Exercise 2.1 Affirmative Simple Past Statements: Regular Verbs

Complete the sentences about The Beatles. Use the simple past form of the verbs in parentheses.

1. The Beatles first _visited_ (visit) the United States in 1964.

2. They ___landed___ (land) in New York on February 7, 1964.

3. The door of the plane ___opened___ (open).

4. The Beatles ___appeared___ (appear).

5. The fans ___cheered___ (cheer) and ___shouted___ (shout).

6. Some fans ___screamed___ (scream) and others ___cried___ (cry).

7. The Beatles ___played___ (play) on *The Ed Sullivan Show* on TV.

8. About 74 million people (over 40 percent of the country) ___watched___ (watch) the show.

9. Their long hair ___shocked___ (shock) the country.

10. They ___changed___ (change) popular music forever.

Exercise 2.2 Negative Simple Past Statements: Regular Verbs

A Complete the first paragraph of this biography with negative simple past verbs. Use the full form *did not*.

This child _did not talk_ (talk) before the age of
(1)
four. He _did not learn_ (learn) to read before the age
(2)
of seven. He _did not like_ (like) his high school, and
(3)
he _did not pass_ (pass) the entrance exam for the
(4)
Swiss Federal Polytechnic School, a university in Zurich.
One teacher _did not believe_ (believe) that he was
(5)
intelligent at all. However, this boy _did not stop_
(6)
(stop) working hard. His teachers _did not recognize_
(7)
(recognize) his genius, but he _did not listen_ (listen)
(8)
to their discouraging words.

B Complete the rest of the biography with simple past forms of the verbs in the box.

enjoy	explain	~~not perform~~	study
enter	graduate	show	work

He _did not perform_ well in school, but he _____ an interest in
(1)   (2)
science, and he _____ math. He _____ for a high school
(3)   (4)
diploma, and finally he _____ the university. He _____ four
(5)   (6)
years later and then _____ on a Ph.D. He later _____ the laws
(7)   (8)
of the universe. Who is he? _____ [The answer is on page 144.]

Exercise 2.3 🔊 Pronunciation Focus: Saying Simple Past Verbs

When the verb ends in /t/ or /d/, say -ed as an extra syllable /ɪd/ or /əd/.	**/ɪd/ or /əd/** /t/ wai**t** → waited /d/ deci**de** → decided
When the verb ends in /f/, /k/, /p/, /s/, /ʃ/, and /tʃ/, say -ed as /t/.	**/t/** /f/ lau**gh** → laughed /s/ mi**ss** → missed /k/ loo**k** → looked /ʃ/ fini**sh** → finished /p/ sto**p** → stopped /tʃ/ wat**ch** → watched
For verbs that end in other consonant and vowel sounds, say -ed as /d/.	**/d/** lis**ten** → listened pl**ay** → played cha**nge** → changed agr**ee** → agreed li**ve** → lived borr**ow** → borrowed

A 🔊 Listen and repeat the verbs in the chart above.

B *Pair Work* Add simple past endings to the verbs below. Then read the sentences aloud with a partner. Do the verbs have an extra syllable? Check (✓) *Yes* or *No*.

	Yes	No
1. A friend **call**_ed_ me last night.		✓
2. I **invite**_d_ her to dinner.	✓	
3. We **talk**____ about music.		
4. She **want**____ to get an old album from the 1960s for her grandfather.		
5. We **surf**____ the Internet.		
6. We **look**____ for the album.		
7. I **download**____ the music files.		
8. We **play**____ them.		
9. They **sound**____ funny.		
10. We **forward**____ the music files to her grandfather.		
11. He **listen**____ to the songs.		
12. Then he **delete**____ them. Not all music from the 1960s is good.		

C *Over to You* Tell a partner about four things you did last night. Use some of the verbs in A.

I watched TV last night.

Exercise 2.4 Vocabulary Focus: Time Expressions

yesterday	*last ...*	*...ago*	**Prepositions**
yesterday	last night	two days ago	in 2007
yesterday morning	last week/month/	six weeks ago	on June 19
yesterday evening	year	10 months/years ago	at 7:30
	last Friday/June/	a long time ago	before/after the
	spring		audition

Time expressions usually come at the end of a sentence.	I listened to a Beatles album **last night**. The Beatles became famous **in 1962**.
Time expressions can also come at the start of a sentence when they are very important.	**After the audition**, they went home and waited. **In 1961**, a record company executive traveled to Liverpool.

Complete the sentences about a famous poet. Use the words from the box. Some words are used more than once.

after	ago	in	last	on

1. I borrowed a book of poems from the library _last_ week.

2. The poet lived in Massachusetts over 100 years _____.

3. She published only seven poems _____ her lifetime.

4. She died at the age of 55 _____ May 15, 1886.

5. _____ the poet's death, her sister discovered over 1,800 poems in her room.

6. Her first book of poems appeared four years after she died, _____ 1890.

7. T. H. Johnson published a complete collection of her poems _____ 1955.

8. I prepared a presentation about her for class _____ night.

1830–1886

Exercise 2.5 Time Expressions

Pair Work When was the last time you or a friend did these things? Ask and answer questions with a partner. Write sentences about your partner.

1. borrow a book from the library _Marie borrowed a book from the library three weeks ago._

2. listen to an MP3 player _____

3. laugh or cry at a movie _____

4. move to another apartment or house _____

5. try really hard to do something _____

6. travel to another city _____

Exercise 2.6 *Did Not* and *Didn't* in Writing

Data from the Real World

Didn't or **Did Not**?		**Didn't** and **Did Not** Compared
People use *didn't* in speaking and informal writing.	*Hey! You **didn't** call yesterday!*	
They use *did not* in formal writing.	*The audition **did not** go well.*	

Rewrite these sentences about the famous poet Emily Dickinson for academic writing. Change the contractions.

1. Emily Dickinson didn't publish a lot of poems in her lifetime.

    Emily Dickinson did not publish a lot of poems in her lifetime.

2. Even her family didn't know about the 1,800 poems in her room.

    _____

3. In the nineteenth century, some critics didn't like her work, but she continued to write for herself.

    _____

4. She didn't write like other poets.

    _____

5. She didn't use correct punctuation.

    _____

6. In the 1950s, poetry experts published her work again. This time, they didn't edit it.

    _____

3 | Simple Past Statements: Irregular Verbs

▶ Grammar Presentation

Irregular simple past verbs don't end in *-ed*.	In 1961, he **went** to Liverpool. The company **made** a big mistake.

3.1 Irregular Verbs

AFFIRMATIVE STATEMENTS

Subject	Simple Past Irregular Verb	
I You We They He / She / It	**became**	popular.

NEGATIVE STATEMENTS

Subject	*Did + Not*	Base Form of Verb	
I You We They He / She / It	**did not** **didn't**	**become**	popular.

3.2 Using Irregular Simple Past Verbs

a. 🌐 Here are the most common irregular verbs.	come → came make → made do → did put → put get → got read → read go → went say → said have → had see → saw
b. Be careful with the verb *do*.	I **did** my homework last night. I **didn't do** my homework this morning.

▸▸ Irregular Verbs: See page A16.

▶ Grammar Application

Exercise 3.1 Simple Past Statements with Irregular Verbs

A Make guesses about things your partner did yesterday. Use the verbs in parentheses. Write affirmative and negative sentences.

1. You _____ *didn't do* _____ (do) your homework last night.
2. You _____ read _____ (read) your e-mail after dinner.
3. You _____ didn't get up (get up) late yesterday morning.
4. You _____ came _____ (come) to school early today.
5. You _____ didn't go _____ (go) to work last night.
6. You _____ made _____ (make) a wonderful dinner yesterday.
7. You _____ didn't see (see) a movie in a theater last weekend.
8. You _____ didn't read (read) a newspaper this morning.
9. You _____ had _____ (have) breakfast this morning.
10. You _____ didn't see (see) the weather report on TV this morning.

B *Pair Work* Read the sentences to your partner. Are your guesses correct?

A *You didn't do your homework last night.*
B *That's true. I did my homework this morning! / That's not true. I did my homework after dinner.*

Exercise 3.2 ◀)) Pronunciation Focus: Saying Irregular Simple Past Verbs

Sometimes the spelling of two verbs is the same, or similar, but the pronunciation is different.	read → read say → said BUT pay → paid hear → heard
Sometimes the letters *gh* are not pronounced.	buy → bought think → thought

When you learn an irregular verb, learn the pronunciation, too.

A ◀)) Listen and repeat the verbs in the chart above. Notice the pronunciation of the irregular past forms.

B Tell a partner about something . . .

1. you bought last week.
2. you read recently.
3. your teacher said in the last class.
4. you thought about today.
5. you paid a lot of money for years ago.
6. you heard on the news today.

Exercise 3.3 More Irregular Simple Past Verbs

A Complete the descriptions with the verbs below. Can you match the pictures to the texts?

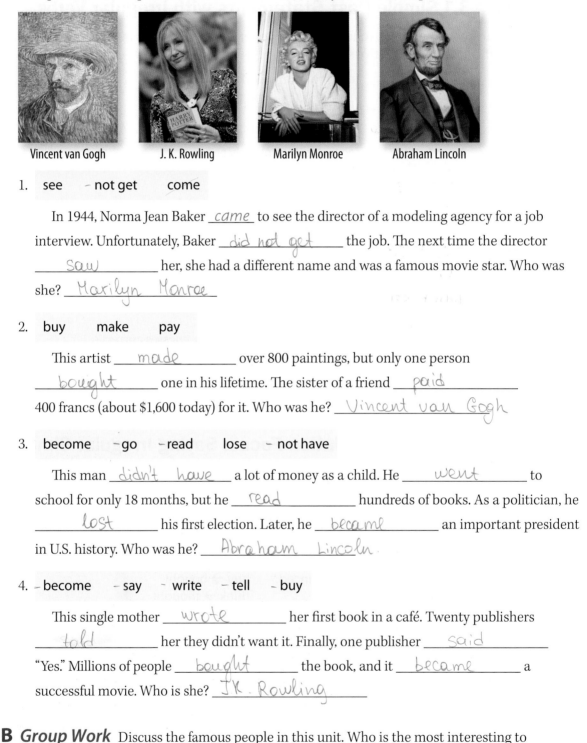

| Vincent van Gogh | J. K. Rowling | Marilyn Monroe | Abraham Lincoln |

1. see   - not get   come

   In 1944, Norma Jean Baker _came_ to see the director of a modeling agency for a job interview. Unfortunately, Baker _did not get_ the job. The next time the director _saw_ her, she had a different name and was a famous movie star. Who was she? _Marilyn Monroe_

2. buy   make   pay

   This artist _made_ over 800 paintings, but only one person _bought_ one in his lifetime. The sister of a friend _paid_ 400 francs (about $1,600 today) for it. Who was he? _Vincent van Gogh_

3. become   - go   - read   lose   - not have

   This man _didn't have_ a lot of money as a child. He _went_ to school for only 18 months, but he _read_ hundreds of books. As a politician, he _lost_ his first election. Later, he _became_ an important president in U.S. history. Who was he? _Abraham Lincoln_

4. - become   - say   - write   - tell   - buy

   This single mother _wrote_ her first book in a café. Twenty publishers _told_ her they didn't want it. Finally, one publisher _said_ "Yes." Millions of people _bought_ the book, and it _became_ a successful movie. Who is she? _J.K. Rowling_

B *Group Work* Discuss the famous people in this unit. Who is the most interesting to you? Why?

Answer to Exercise 2.2B, p. 138: Albert Einstein

4 Avoid Common Mistakes ⚠

1. Use simple past verbs to write or talk about the past.

started
He ~~starts~~ his career in 2002.

ate
I ~~eat~~ at a restaurant last night.

2. After *did not / didn't*, use the base form of the verb. Do <u>not</u> use the past form.

earn
They didn't ~~earned~~ a lot of money.

3. For the negative, write *did not* as two words.

did not
She ~~didnot~~ get the job.

4. Use the correct spelling for simple past verbs.

bought	*took*	*read*	*studied*	*dropped*	*paid*
~~buyed~~	~~taked~~	~~red~~	~~studyed~~	~~droped~~	~~payed~~

5. The simple past negative of *have* is *did not / didn't have*. The simple past negative of *do* is *did not / didn't do*.

didn't have
He ~~had not~~ a successful career.

did not do
She ~~did not~~ her homework last night.

Editing Task

Find and correct ten more mistakes in this paragraph about the inventor of the lightbulb.

did not have
Thomas Edison was born in 1847 in Milan, Ohio. He ~~had not~~ very much education in school. His mother taught him reading, writing, and math. Like many children at the time, he droped out of school and got a job. At age 13, he sells newspapers and candy at a railroad station. Thomas

5 continue to learn about science by reading. At age 16, he become a telegraph operator.[1] Later he start to invent things. In 1869, he moved to New York City. One of his inventions earned him $40,000, so he opened his first research laboratory[2] in New Jersey. He tried hundreds of times to make the first lightbulb, but he had not success. However, Thomas Edison didnot give up. He learn from his mistakes. In 1879, he introduce

10 his greatest invention, the electric light for the home. He told a reporter, "I didn't failed 1,000 times. The lightbulb was an invention with 1,000 steps."

[1]**telegraph operator:** a person who worked with a communication device that sent and received signals | [2]**research laboratory:** a building with equipment for doing scientific tests

5 | Grammar for Writing

Writing About People in the Past

Writers use the simple past to describe specific events and repeated events in a person's life. Remember:

- **Use the simple past with time expressions to tell the order of events in stories.**
  Twenty-five years ago, Jenna wrote an important letter. She waited a long time, but after six months, she got an answer to her letter.

- **Many verbs are irregular, and there are many ways to spell irregular verbs.**
  He had three different jobs one year.   They went to school at night.

Pre-writing Task

1 Read the paragraph about an immigrant from Vietnam. How was he successful?

A Success Story

In 1996, Tam left Vietnam and came to the United States. Life was difficult in the beginning because he didn't speak English. He took English classes at night and looked for jobs during the day. He did not find a job at first, but after
5 several months, he found a good job at a local grocery store. Tam was very hardworking, and he learned the business very quickly. After a few years, the store owners gave Tam the job of manager. In 2002, the owners retired. Tam bought the store. The store is a very popular place in our neighborhood.
10 Tam's story is a good success story.

2 Read the paragraph again. Circle the regular past tense verbs and underline the irregular past tense verbs. Then double underline the time phrases. Notice how the time expressions tell the order of events in the story.

Writing Task

1 *Write* Use the paragraph in the Pre-writing Task to help you write a paragraph about a success story you know. What happened in this person's life? Use time expressions to tell the order of the events. Explain why the person is successful. You can write about a person you know or about the life of someone well known on the Internet. Use time expressions such as:

- In (year), he / she _____.
- Later, he / she _____.
- After (period of time), he / she _____.

2 *Self-Edit* Use the editing tips below to improve your sentences. Make any necessary changes.

1. Did you use the simple past to describe the person's success story?
2. Did you use time expressions to explain the order of events in the story?
3. Did you check the form and spelling of the simple past forms of your verbs?
4. Did you avoid the mistakes in the Avoid Common Mistakes chart on page 145?

1 | Grammar in the Real World

A Do you know a business owner? Read the conversation between two students below.
What is unusual about Blake Mycoskie's business?

Greg Hey, Liliana. **Did you finish** your report for class
tomorrow?

Liliana No, but I found a really interesting businessman,
Blake Mycoskie. Do you remember him from that
5   reality TV show, *The Amazing Race*?

Greg No, not really. **Did he win?**

Liliana No, he didn't, but that's not important. My report is
on his *business*. It's really unusual.

Greg Why? **What did he do?** Let me guess. . . . He started
10   a cool company, and he made millions from his idea.

Liliana He started a cool company, and it helps fight
poverty. He sells shoes, and . . .

Greg **Did you say** "shoes"?

Liliana Yes, he started TOMS Shoes in 2006. For every pair of shoes he sells, he donates
15   a pair to a child in need.[1] By the end of September 2010, he distributed[2] his one
millionth pair.

Greg Hmm. Interesting. But **why did he decide to sell shoes?**

Liliana During *The Amazing Race*, he traveled with his sister all over the world. He saw a
lot of very poor people and lots of children without shoes. A lot of these children
20   had diseases because they walked barefoot.[3] The schools did not allow children
to attend without shoes. So he came up with this concept[4] of selling and donating
shoes. In the future, he plans to expand[5] his business and make other products, too.

Greg Oh, I see. He's a social entrepreneur. He wants to make money, but he also wants to
help people.

[1]**in need:** not having enough money | [2]**distribute:** give something to many people | [3]**barefoot:** not wearing any shoes or socks |
[4]**concept:** idea | [5]**expand:** make something bigger

B *Comprehension Check* Answer the questions.

1. Did Blake Mycoskie win *The Amazing Race* on TV? _____

2. When did he start TOMS Shoes? _____

3. How many pairs of shoes did he distribute by the end of September 2010? _____

4. What are two problems for children without shoes? _____

C *Notice* Find the questions in the conversation. Complete the questions.

1. Did you _finish_ your report for class tomorrow?

2. What did he _do yesterday_ ?

3. Did you _say_ "shoes"?

4. Why did he _decide_ to sell shoes?

What form of the verb did you use to complete the questions?

2 | Simple Past *Yes / No* Questions

▶ Grammar Presentation

Simple past *Yes / No* questions ask about actions and events that happened before now.	*Did* you **finish** your report? *Did* he **win** the competition?

2.1 *Yes / No* Questions

Did	Subject	Base Form of Verb	
Did	I you we they he / she / it	**finish**	the report?

2.2 Short Answers

AFFIRMATIVE				NEGATIVE		
	Yes	Subject	*Did*	*No*	Subject	*Did + Not*
	Yes,	I you we they he / she / it	**did.**	**No,**	I you we they he / she / it	**did not.** **didn't.**

2.3 Using Simple Past *Yes / No* Questions

a. Questions in the simple past often use definite past-time expressions.	*Did Blake go to college **in the 1990s**?* *Did he start his company **11 years ago**?*
b. Use the contraction *didn't* in negative short answers. The full form *did not* is very formal.	*"Did Blake win* The Amazing Race?" *"No, he **didn't**."*
c. Use pronouns in short answers.	*"Did Blake start a shoe company?"* *"Yes, **he** did."*
To give extra information, you can also answer *Yes / No* questions with long answers.	*"Yes, **he started TOMS shoes in 2006**."*

▶ # Grammar Application

Exercise 2.1 Simple Past *Yes / No* Questions

Liliana heard about Blake Mycoskie and then went to a trade show[1] for entrepreneurs. Complete the questions in the simple past. Use the words in parentheses.

Liliana   <u>Did you have</u> (you / have) a
               (1)
good weekend?

Simon   Yeah, pretty good. How about you?

Liliana   Yes, very good.

Simon   _____ (you / go out)?
               (2)

Liliana   Yeah. I went out with Aisha on Saturday.

Simon   Oh, _____ (you / go)
               (3)
somewhere interesting?

Liliana   Yeah. We went to a trade show. There were lots of exhibits[2] from new companies.

Simon   A trade show? I didn't know you were interested in business!

Liliana   Yes, I'm very interested in it. _____ (I / tell) you about my
               (4)
grandmother's company?

Simon   No.

Liliana   My grandmother had her own clothing design company, so I want to do

something like that.

[1]**trade show:** a large event at which companies show and sell their products and try to increase their business
[2]**exhibit:** a collection of things people can see in public

Simon   Really? _____ (you / see) any design companies there?
                                          (5)

Liliana   Yeah. We saw some. A lot of the companies' owners are young entrepreneurs.

Simon   _____ (you / speak) with any interesting people?
                            (6)

Liliana   Yeah. I spoke with the owner of a men's tie company. He designs his own fabric.[3]

Simon   Hmm. _____ (he / have) any good ideas for you?
                                    (7)

Liliana   Yes. He told me one thing: find a good business partner. What do you say?

Do you want to be my business partner?

[3]**fabric:** cloth or material

Exercise 2.2 Simple Past Yes / No Questions and Answers

A Read Liliana's notes for her report on Blake Mycoskie. Then write the questions.

> ## Questions About Blake Mycoskie
>
> 1. Second in "The Amazing Race"?
> 2. Other businesses before TOMS?
> 3. Sister – start the business with him?
> 4. Any experience in fashion?
> 5. Company – difficulties at the beginning?

1. he / finish _Did he finish second in "The Amazing Race"?_ _____

2. he / have _____

3. his sister / start _____

4. he / have _____

5. the company / have _____

B Read some more information about Blake. Then answer the questions in A. First, write one short answer, and then write one long answer with extra information for each question.

When Blake Mycoskie competed in *The Amazing Race* with his sister Paige, they finished third. They lost the race by only four minutes. His sister helped him with the concept of TOMS Shoes, but he started the business by himself. He had previous experience in business, but he didn't have any experience in fashion. But he liked to design things. Before TOMS shoes, he started five other businesses, including a college laundry business and a reality TV channel. When he started TOMS, he had a lot of problems with the shoe factory.[1] Now the factory runs well, and a lot of people work for him.

[1]**factory:** a building where people use machines to produce things

1. a. *No, he didn't.*
   b. *No, he finished third.*
2. a. _____
   b. _____
3. a. _____
   b. _____
4. a. _____
   b. _____
5. a. _____
   b. _____

C *Pair Work* Ask and answer the questions about Blake with a partner.

Exercise 2.3 More Simple Past Yes/No Questions and Answers

A *Over to You* Write questions to ask a partner about last weekend. For question 5, use your own verb.

1. (do) *Did you do anything interesting?*
2. (work) *Did you work yesterday?*
3. (have) *What did you have a grammar book?*
4. (go out) *Did you go out on Wednesday?*
5. *What did you do on Monday?*

B *Pair Work* Ask and answer the questions with your partner. Give your partner additional information.

A *Did you do anything interesting?*
B *No, not really. I stayed home.*

A *Did you go out on Saturday?*
B *Yes, I went to . . . ./No, I worked all day.*

3 | Simple Past Information Questions

▶ Grammar Presentation

Simple past information questions ask about people, things, times, places, etc., that happened before now.

What did he **do?**
Why did he **decide** to make shoes?

3.1 Information Questions

Wh- Word	Did	Subject	Base Form of Verb	
Who			write	about?
What		I	do	yesterday?
When		you	finish	our report?
What time	did	we they	begin	writing?
Where		he	visit	on vacation?
Why		she it	start	a company?
How			save	enough money?

3.2 Using Simple Past Information Questions

a. Use simple past information questions to ask for specific information about something that happened in the past.

"**Where did** she **study** business?"
"She studied at Florida State."
"**When did** she **graduate**?"
"She graduated in 2012."

b. Use Wh- words with did to ask about habits and regular activities.

"**What did** she **do** every summer?"
"She worked at a restaurant."

3.3 Using Wh- Words in Simple Past Information Questions

a. Use Who to ask about people.

Who did you start your company with?

My sister.

b. Use What to ask about things.

What did you make?

Shoes.

c. Use When to ask about time (days, months, years, seasons, parts of the day).

When did you have this idea?

Last week.

3.3 Using *Wh-* Words in Simple Past Information Questions *(continued)*

d. Use *What time* to ask about clock time.	***What time*** *did you start work today?*	*At seven o'clock.*
e. Use *Where* to ask about places.	***Where*** *did you go to business school?*	*In Boston.*
f. Use *Why* to ask about reasons.	***Why*** *did you open a restaurant?*	*Because I love food.*
g. Use *How* to ask about manner.	***How*** *did you save enough money?*	*I saved some every month.*

▶ # Grammar Application

Exercise 3.1 Simple Past Information Questions and Answers

A Shelly Hwang, an entrepreneur, started a chain of frozen yogurt stores called Pinkberry. Unscramble the words to make questions about her.

Shelly Hwang, founder of Pinkberry

1. Why / she / to / move / did / the United States?
   Why did she move to the United States?

2. What / after / she / did / college? / do
   _____

3. Who / she / with? / develop / the concept / did
   _____

4. When / open / store? / she / did / her first
   _____

5. What / have? / the store / did / flavors
   _____

B ◀)) Listen to an instructor talk about Hwang. Then write short answers to the questions in A.

1. _To study business._____   4. _____

2. _____   5. _____

3. _____

4 Avoid Common Mistakes ⚠

1. Use *did* + subject + base form of the verb.

      did   *graduate*
When you ~~graduated~~ from business school?

2. In information questions, use *did* and the base form of the main verb. Do <u>not</u> use the past form.

          open   *become*
Where did you ~~opened~~ the first store? Did it ~~became~~ a success?

3. When *do* is the main verb, use *did* + subject + *do* (base form of verb).

          do
What did you at the company?

Editing Task

Find and correct the mistakes in these questions about your work experience.

       work

1. Did you ~~worked~~ for a relative?

2. Who you worked for?

3. What did you?

4. How many hours did you worked each week?

5. How much money did you earned each week?

6. You enjoyed your job?

7. What you learned from this job?

8. Why did you stopped working?

5 | Grammar for Writing ✐

Writing Questions About People's Activities in the Past

Writers use questions in the simple past to get specific information about the topic or person they want to write about. They use *Yes / No* and information questions together to help them get all the information they need.

Remember:

Question word order for *Yes / No* questions and for information questions is similar.

<u>Did Mira work</u> at her organization at night?

<u>Where did Mira work</u> during the daytime? (at which organization?)

Pre-writing Task

1 Read the interview questions and answers about Aunt Liz. Then read the paragraph a student wrote about her. Why does the student admire Aunt Liz?

1. *A* (What) did you <u>do</u>?
   B I took care of my parents – your grandparents – when they were sick.

2. *A* Why did you do this?
   B I helped them because they needed help. They were too sick to cook or even go to their doctors' appointments.

3. *A* When did you do this?
   B This happened last year when they had the flu.

4. *A* How did you do this?
   B I went to their house every day and did what they needed.

5. *A* Did you work at the same time?
   B Yes. I went to their house after my own work.

6. *A* Did you ever complain?
   B No, I didn't. Why should I complain? I am healthy and they're my parents.

Amazing Aunt Liz

My Aunt Liz is an outstanding person. She cares about people a lot, and she always helps people. Last year, both my grandparents got sick, and Aunt Liz took care of them. The whole family helped, but my Aunt Liz did most of the work. She went to their house every day after work. She cooked their meals, and she cleaned their house. She often drove my grandparents to doctors' appointments. She got very tired, but she didn't complain. My grandparents are well now because of Aunt Liz.

2 Read the interview questions again. Circle the question words and underline the main verb.

Writing Task

1 *Write* Use the questions and paragraph in the Pre-writing Task to help you write interview questions about a person you admire or who did something important. Ask for specific information about the person. You can write about a person you know or find out about a famous person on the Internet.

2 *Self-Edit* Use the editing tips below to improve your sentences. Make any necessary changes.

1. Did you use *Yes / No* and information questions to get specific information about the person you admire?
2. Did you use the correct word order for *Yes / No* and information questions?
3. Did you avoid the mistakes in the Avoid Common Mistakes chart on page 155?

Simple Past of *Be*

Life Stories

1 Grammar in the Real World

A What were you like as a child? Read the magazine article about Bill Gates. What was he like as a child?

Bill Gates

Bill Gates started the software[1] company Microsoft, and it is now one of the computer giants[2] of the world. However, Bill started his life in an ordinary family. He **was** born in Seattle,
5 Washington, in 1955. His father **was** a lawyer. His mother did volunteer work in the community. Bill **was** the second of three children in the Gates family: Bill, his sister Kristianne, and his sister Libby. They **were** all very intelligent children.

10 When Bill **was** about 12 years old, his parents began to worry about him. He **was** a good student, but life **was** not perfect at home. Bill **was** bored, and he often argued with his family. Eventually, his parents sent him to a new school. This **was** an important step for Bill because in this new school, there **were** some computers. Bill began to learn about computers, and he loved them. He and his
15 friends spent many hours on them. Bill also began to write software programs. In the new school, he **was** active and busy, and he **was** happy.

After high school, Bill went to Harvard University, but he **was** in the computer lab a lot and didn't go to class all the time. After one year, he left Harvard and formed a software company with his friend Paul Allen. Their
20 company later became Microsoft.

[1]**software:** computer programs | [2]**giant:** a very large or powerful organization

B *Comprehension Check* Do these words describe Bill Gates as a child or as an adult? Check (✔) the correct answers. Some words describe both. Use the article to help you.

	As a Child	As an Adult
1. head of a computer giant	☐	☐
2. bored	☐	☐
3. intelligent	☐	☐
4. a good student	☐	☐

C *Notice* Read the sentences. Circle *was* or *were*. Use the article to help you.

1. His father **was** / **were** a lawyer.
2. They **was** / **were** all very intelligent children.
3. This **was** / **were** an important step for Bill.
4. Bill **was** / **were** the second of three children.
5. There **was** / **were** some computers.
6. Life **was** / **were** not perfect at home.

When do you use *was*? When do you use *were*?

2 | Simple Past of *Be*: Affirmative and Negative Statements

▶ Grammar Presentation

The simple past of *be* describes people, places, or things in the past.	*His home **was** in Seattle, Washington.* *He and his sisters **were** good students.*

2.1 Statements

AFFIRMATIVE			NEGATIVE		
Subject	***Was / Were***		**Subject**	***Was / Were* + *Not***	
I He She It	**was**	in the computer lab.	I He She It	**was not** **wasn't**	in class.
We You They	**were**		We You They	**were not** **weren't**	

2.2 Using Simple Past of *Be*

a. Use the simple past of *be* to talk or write about people, places, or things in the past. *Be* has two past forms: *was* and *were*.	He **was** a lawyer. The students **were** in their class. I **was not** in the computer lab. They **were not** bored.
b. Use *was / were + born* to say when or where someone was born.	He **was born** in Seattle, Washington, in 1955.
c. *Not* comes after *be* in negative statements.	He was a good student, but life **was not** perfect at home.
d. In speaking, you can use the contractions *wasn't* and *weren't* in negative statements.	Bill **wasn't** interested in school. They **weren't** wealthy.
e. We often use past time expressions with the simple past of *be*: *ten years ago / yesterday / this morning / last week / in the past* Past time expressions can go either at the beginning of a sentence or at the end of a sentence.	**In 1973**, Bill **was** a student at Harvard. We **were** in Seattle **last week**.

▶ # Grammar Application

Exercise 2.1 Simple Past of *Be*: Affirmative and Negative Statements

A Read the descriptions of three famous women. Complete the sentences with *was / wasn't* or *were / weren't*. Write the names on the lines.

Oprah Winfrey	Taylor Swift	Penélope Cruz

1. ___Penélope Cruz___

   She __*was*__ born in Madrid, Spain, in 1974. Her father
   (1)
   __was__ an auto mechanic[1] and her mother __was__
   (2)   (3)
   a hairdresser.[2] She studied ballet and jazz dance as a child.

   When she __was__ a teenager, she started acting. At 17,
   (4)
   she __was__ in her first film.
   (5)

   [1]**auto mechanic:** someone who repairs cars | [2]**hairdresser:** a person who cuts and styles hair (usually women's hair)

2. _____

    She _____ born in Mississippi in 1954. Her mother
         (6)
and father _____ very poor. Her father _____ a
         (7)   (8)
barber.[3] When she _____ in high school, she got her
              (9)
first radio job. She _____ a student at Tennessee State
             (10)
University for several years. She got her first TV job in 1972.
By age 32, she _____ a millionaire.
           (11)

[3]**barber:** a person who cuts men's hair

3. _____

    She _____ born in Pennsylvania in 1989. As a child,
        (12)
she loved to write and wrote in her diary every day. When she

_____ in the fourth grade, she won a poetry contest.[4] She
   (13)
began to write songs, and she sang at festivals and contests.
She _____ (not) shy, and she liked to perform. In high
     (14)
school, she _____ (not) very popular. Other students
        (15)
_____ (not) friendly with her. Now she's very popular.
 (16)

[4]**contest:** a competition to win a prize

B Complete the sentences with *was* and *wasn't*. Use the information in A to help you.

1. Penélope Cruz _*wasn't*_ born in the United States.

2. As a child, Taylor Swift _____ a songwriter.

3. Oprah Winfrey's family _____ wealthy.

4. As a child, Penélope Cruz _____ a dancer.

5. By age 32, Oprah Winfrey _____ poor.

6. Oprah Winfrey's father _____ a TV star.

7. Penélope Cruz _____ a teenager when she started acting.

e. Use *Where* to ask about places.	***Where*** were you born?	*In Tokyo.*
f. Use *Why* to ask about reasons.	***Why*** were they excited?	*Because they won the game.*
g. Use *How* to ask what something was like.	***How*** was the play?	*It was great.*
h. Use *How old* to ask about age.	***How old*** was your brother last year?	*He was 18.*

▶ # Grammar Application

Exercise 3.1 Simple Past of *Be*: Yes / No Questions

A Tanya's class assignment is to interview her grandfather. Complete her questions with *Was* or *Were*.

1. _____*Were*_____ you born in New York City?

2. _____ your family large?

3. _____ your brother a good student?

4. _____ you and your brother good friends?

5. _____ your sisters nice to you?

6. _____ you and your sisters the same age?

7. _____ your father's store near the house?

B 🔊 ***Pair Work*** Listen to the conversation between Tanya and her grandfather. Write short answers about the grandfather's life to the questions in A. Then compare your answers with a partner.

1. _No, he wasn't._ _____

2. _____

3. _____

4. _____

5. _____

6. _____

7. _____

Exercise 3.2 Simple Past of *Be*: Yes / No Questions and Information Questions

A Read the paragraph about a childhood photograph. Then write information questions and answers about the photograph.

My great-grandmother was born in 1901 in Wisconsin. She was born at 12:10 in the morning. She was the first of two children. Her father was a store owner, and her mother was a teacher. They lived in a small town. I once saw a

5 photograph of her house. The house had two floors, and it was very simple. There was no paint on the house, but it was well built. There was a nice front porch with several chairs and some flowers. My great-grandmother and her father were in the photo. Her father was happy, but she was angry

10 because she hated sitting for pictures. She was about three years old in the photo. She was upset but very cute.

1. (When / she born)

   When was she born?   _She was born in 1901._

2. (Where / she born)

   _____   _____

3. (What time / she born)

   _____   _____

4. (What / her father's job)

   _____   _____

5. (What / her mother's job)

   _____   _____

6. (Who / in the photo)

   _____   _____

7. (What / on the porch)

   _____   _____

8. (Why / she angry)

   _____   _____

9. (How old / she in the photo)

   _____   _____

B *Over to You* Write questions to ask a partner about his or her childhood. Write *Yes / No* questions and information questions. Use *was / were* and the words in the box or your own ideas.

born	favorite family activity	school
brothers	favorite games	sisters
chores[1]	favorite room in your house	your bedroom
father's / mother's job	favorite toys	

Where were you born?

1. _____

2. _____

3. _____

4. _____

5. _____

6. _____

7. _____

8. _____

[1]**chore:** a job that is often boring but that is important, like washing the dishes

C *Pair Work* Ask and answer the questions about childhood from B. Take turns.

A Were you born in the United States?
B No, I was born in Thailand.

4 Avoid Common Mistakes ⚠

1. With *I* / *he* / *she* / *it* or a singular noun, use *was*.

He ~~were~~ a famous artist. *(was)*

2. With *you* / *we* / *they* or a plural noun, use *were*.

My brothers ~~was~~ usually nice to me. *(were)*

3. Use the correct form with *born*.

When ~~was you born?~~ *(were you born)*   I ~~born~~ in 1980. *(was born)*

Editing Task

Find and correct seven more mistakes in the questions and answers about Yo-Yo Ma.

A When ~~were~~ Yo-Yo Ma born? *(was)*

B He born in 1955. *(was)*

A He born in the United States? *(Was)*

B No, he wasn't. He was born in France.

5 *A* Were his parents French?

B No, they was not. They was Chinese. *(were)* *(were)*

A Were his parents musicians?

B Yes, they was talented musicians. *(were)*

A How old was he when he first played

10 the cello?

B He was four.

A How old were he when he moved to *(was)*

New York City?

B He were five. *(was)*

15 *A* How many albums does he have?

B Currently, he has more than 75 albums.

Yo-Yo Ma, cellist

5 | Grammar for Writing

Writing About Childhood Memories

Writers often use the simple past of *be* to describe people, places, and things in the past. They use other verbs to explain what happened.
Remember:

- **Use the simple past of *be* for your descriptions of the past.**
  Jai and her brother <u>were</u> very smart. They <u>were</u> good students.

- **Use *There was / There were* to show what things or places were like.**
  <u>There was</u> always a lot to do in their neighborhood. <u>There were</u> always other neighborhood children around to play with.

Pre-writing Task

1 Read the paragraph from a student. What did the writer's mother do, and why was it difficult for her?

A Difficult Moment

   My mother <u>was</u> always a great singer. When she was 12, (there was) a talent competition at her school. My mother <u>registered</u> to sing in the show. She was very nervous because it was her first concert. The room was
5 very hot. There were no open windows, and there were many people in the room. My mother did not want to sing because she was scared. Her throat was very dry. Then she saw her parents. They smiled at her, and that helped her. She sang her song. It was great! My mother
10 often talks about this memory.

2 Read the paragraph again. Circle all the examples of *there was / there were*. Underline the past forms of *be* verbs, and <u>double underline</u> the other past forms of verbs.

Writing Task

1 *Write* Use the paragraph in the Pre-writing Task to help you write a paragraph about a childhood experience of another person in your class. Ask a partner to think of a happy, sad, exciting, scary, or proud moment. Then ask that person to tell you about this moment. Ask questions.

Use sentences in your paragraph such as:

- When she / he was _____ years old, she / he _____.
- There were / was _____.
- He / She was very nervous / happy / sad because _____.

2 *Self-Edit* Use the editing tips below to improve your sentences. Make any necessary changes.

1. Did you use the simple past of *be* to describe things and other simple past verbs to tell the story of a special childhood memory?
2. Did you use the simple past of *be* in your descriptions?
3. Did you use *there was / there were* in your descriptions?
4. Did you avoid the mistakes in the Avoid Common Mistakes chart on page 167?

1 Grammar in the Real World

A Do you ever get e-mails with the message, "You won a contest," or "We need to check your bank account"? Read the web article below. Why was Sandra Walters lucky?

Internet Lottery Scam[1]

When Sandra Walters opened her e-mail one day at work last year, she was surprised. One message said, "Congratulations. You are the lucky winner of $2.5 million in the National Millionaire's Contest. Call
5 this number." **When Sandra got home**, she called the number and spoke to a man who seemed very nice. The man told her to send a $1,000 fee[2] to a bank outside the United States. **When Sandra said she didn't have $1,000**, the man said, "No problem. I can
10 charge your credit card." She gave him her credit card number, her bank account number, and her address. The man promised to send her a check for $2.5 million the next day. Then he hung up. **After Sandra put the phone down**, she began to think. What was this
15 contest? She didn't remember entering any contest. How did she win?

Unfortunately, it's a common story. There is no National Millionaire's Contest. In a real contest, you never pay a fee **before you receive your prize**. Sandra wasn't a winner. She was the victim[3] of a scam . . . almost. Luckily, Sandra realized her mistake
20 and called her credit card company. They canceled[4] the card **before the criminals[5] used it**.

Don't fall for[6] this scam. An e-mail message that asks for personal information is probably a scam. Just delete it!

---

[1]**scam:** a dishonest way of making money | [2]**fee:** money you pay for a service | [3]**victim:** someone who suffers from violence, illness, or bad luck | [4]**cancel:** stop something from working | [5]**criminal:** a person who has done something illegal | [6]**fall for:** believe something is true when it's not

B *Comprehension Check* Circle the correct answers.

1. Where did Sandra receive the e-mail?
   a. at home   b. at work   c. at the bank

2. How much money did the man ask her to send to a bank outside the United States?
   a. $1,000   b. $2.5 million   c. $25

3. Why did Sandra give her credit card number to the man?
   a. because she didn't have a bank   b. because it was quick   c. to pay the fee

4. When did she realize it was a scam?
   a. when she got home   b. after she finished the call   c. when she called her credit card company

C *Notice* What did Sandra do first? For each pair of sentences, write *1* and *2*. Use the article to help you.

1. _____ Sandra was surprised.   _____ Sandra read her e-mail.
2. _____ She called the number.   _____ She went home.
3. _____ She said she didn't have $1,000.   _____ The man asked for her credit card number.
4. _____ She began to think.   _____ She put the phone down.
5. _____ She realized her mistake.   _____ She called her credit card company.

2 | Past Time Clauses with *When*, *Before*, and *After*

▶ Grammar Presentation

Time clauses show the order of events in the past. They can begin with *when*, *before*, and *after*.	FIRST EVENT SECOND EVENT ***After Sandra put the phone down,*** *she began to think.*

2.1 Time Clauses

Time Clause		Main Clause	Main Clause	Time Clause	
When **Before** **After**	**I get to work,**	I check my e-mail.	I check my e-mail	**when** **before** **after**	**I get to work.**

2.2 Main Clauses and Time Clauses

a. A clause has a subject and a verb.

SUBJECT VERB
She was surprised.

SUBJECT   VERB
When **Sandra opened** her e-mail, ...

b. A main clause is a complete sentence. It has a subject and a verb.

SUBJECT   VERB
Sandra called the number.

SUBJECT VERB
She began to think.

c. A time clause can begin with *when*, *before*, or *after*. It has a subject and a verb. However, it is <u>not</u> a complete sentence. A time clause always goes with a main clause.

SUBJECT VERB   SUBJECT VERB
When **she got** home, she called the number.

SUBJECT   VERB   SUBJECT VERB
After **Sandra put** the phone down, she began to think.

d. You can add a time clause to a main clause to say when something happened.

MAIN CLAUSE   TIME CLAUSE
Sandra called the number **when she got home**.

TIME CLAUSE   MAIN CLAUSE
After Sandra put the phone down, she began to think.

e. A time clause can go before or after the main clause.
When the time clause comes first, use a comma after it.

TIME CLAUSE   MAIN CLAUSE
When Sandra opened her e-mail, she was surprised.

TIME CLAUSE   MAIN CLAUSE
After Sandra put the phone down, she began to think.

When the time clause comes second, do not use a comma.

MAIN CLAUSE   TIME CLAUSE
Sandra was surprised **when she opened her e-mail**.

MAIN CLAUSE   TIME CLAUSE
Sandra began to think **after she put the phone down**.

Time clauses are more common after the main clause.

MAIN CLAUSE   TIME CLAUSE
They canceled the card **before the criminals used it**.

2.3 Ordering Events

a. *When* means "at almost the same time." Use *when* to introduce the first event.	FIRST EVENT SECOND EVENT **When** Sandra opened her e-mail, she was surprised. SECOND EVENT FIRST EVENT Sandra called the number **when** she got home.
b. Use *after* to introduce the first event.	FIRST EVENT SECOND EVENT **After** Sandra put the phone down, she began to think. SECOND EVENT FIRST EVENT She felt much better **after** she called the bank.
c. Use *before* to introduce the second event.	FIRST EVENT SECOND EVENT She canceled the card **before** they used it. SECOND EVENT FIRST EVENT **Before** they sent her prize, they asked her to pay a fee.
d. *Before* and *after* are also prepositions. You can use them before nouns that do not have verbs after them.	**After work**, she went home. She was so excited **before the phone call**.

▶ Grammar Application

Exercise 2.1 *When, Before,* or *After?*

A Choose the correct words to complete the sentences about the article.

1. Sandra opened her e-mail (**when**)/ **before** she got to work.

2. **When / Before** she read the e-mail, Sandra was surprised.

3. She called the number **after / before** she got home.

4. The man and Sandra talked **before / after** he had her personal bank information.

5. **When / Before** Sandra said she didn't have $1,000, the man asked for her credit card number.

6. She gave him her address **after / before** she read out her credit card number.

7. **After / Before** she put the phone down, Sandra realized her mistake.

8. She called her credit card company **before / after** she spoke to the man.

B *Pair Work* Compare your answers with a partner. Which sentences can use both words?

Exercise 2.2 Ordering Events

A 🔊 Listen to the story about another scam. Number the pictures in the order the events happened.

a. _____

He bought a
newspaper.

b. _____

_____

c. _____

_____

d. _____

_____

e. __1__

_____

f. _____

_____

B Write the sentences under the correct pictures in A.

~~He bought a newspaper.~~   He left for work.

He read an e-mail from the bank.   He wrote a note to his wife.

He met a co-worker on the train.   He called his wife.

C 🔊) Complete the story with *when*, *before*, and *after*. Then listen again to check your answers.

About a year ago, my friend Leo was almost a scam victim. One morning, he saw an e-mail from his bank _*before*_ he went to work. _____ he opened the

(1)

(2)

e-mail, it said, "You have a new account number. Write your old account number here so we can check your identity." He didn't have time to reply _____ he left home.

(3)

_____ he left for work, he wrote a

(4)

note to his wife, "Please reply to the bank's e-mail." Then he left for work.

_____ he got to the subway station, he bought a newspaper.

(5)

_____ he got on the train, he met a co-worker and they talked.

(6)

_____ he read the newspaper at lunchtime, he read an article about a bank

(7)

Internet scam. He realized the e-mail from the bank was that scam. _____

(8)

he read the article, he called his wife. Luckily, _____ his wife read the

(9)

e-mail, she realized it was a scam and deleted the e-mail.

Exercise 2.3 Writing Main Clauses and Time Clauses

A *Over to You* What did you do yesterday? Complete each sentence by adding a main clause with a subject and a verb. For sentences with the time clause first, use a comma.

1. _____ before I left home yesterday morning.

2. After I ate lunch _____ .

3. Before I went home last night _____ .

4. _____ when I got home last night.

5. _____ after I ate dinner.

6. Before I went to bed _____ .

B *Over to You* What did you do today? Complete each sentence by adding a time clause with *when*, *before*, or *after*. For sentences with the time clause first, use a comma.

1. I got dressed _____ .

2. _____ I brushed my teeth.

3. I left the house / apartment _____ .

4. I got to school _____ .

5. _____ I went to the classroom.

6. _____ my English class started.

C *Pair Work* Share your sentences with a partner. Did you do any of the same things?

Exercise 2.4 More Main Clauses and Time Clauses

Pair Work Tell a story about a scam from this unit or use your own ideas. First make notes to help you. Then share your story with a partner. Ask questions about your partner's scam story.

A *This happened to a friend last year. When she checked her e-mail, she saw a message from a stranger.*

B *What did it say?*

3 | Avoid Common Mistakes ⚠

1. Check the spelling of *when*, *before*, and *after*.

When
~~Whin~~ she read the e-mail, she got excited.   They canceled the card ~~befor~~ *before* the criminals used it.

after
She thought about it ~~afther~~ she put the phone down.

2. When the time clause comes first, use a comma. Don't use a comma when the main clause comes first.

When she got home⌄she called the company.   She called the company⧸when she got home.

3. Don't forget the subject in the main clause and the time clause.

she
Before Ana called the company,⌄checked the address.

Ana
Before⌄called the company, she checked the address.

Editing Task

Find and correct 13 more mistakes in this story about a scam.

When ⌄*I* got home one night two months ago I had a voice-mail message. When I

listened to the message, got excited. The message said, "Congratulations. You are a

winner in our contest." Befor I made dinner, called the number. A woman said, "We

called you two weeks ago, but you didn't answer. Please hold." After waited for an

5 hour, I put the phone down.

Whin my wife got home I asked her, "Did you get a message about a prize

drawing?" She said, "Yes, but afther heard it, I deleted it. It's a scam." When she said that

I didn't say anything.

I realized my mistake, when we got the phone bill four days later. When read

10 the bill I didn't believe it. That one-hour call cost $5,000!

4 | Grammar for Writing

Telling Stories

Writers often use time clauses with *when*, *before*, and *after* when they tell a story or write about something that happened. Time clauses help the reader understand the order of events. Remember:

- **Use *when* to introduce an event that happened at the same time as another event, *before* to introduce an event that happened after another event, and *after* to introduce the first event that happened.**

  Milton looked up <u>*when*</u> *Heidi walked in the room.*
  <u>*Before*</u> *she spoke to Milton, Heidi sat down.* <u>*After*</u> *she sat down, Milton said hello to her.*

- **When you use a time clause, always use a main clause.**

  TIME CLAUSE   MAIN CLAUSE
  When he opened his messages, he got a big surprise.

Pre-writing Task

1 Read the paragraph below. What was so bad about the writer's morning?

A Terrible Morning

    I had a terrible morning last week. Many things went wrong. I grabbed my coffee ¹ (before) I left to ² catch the bus. When I got ✓ on the bus, I didn't have ✓ my bus pass. I paid the driver with cash and sat down. After I put my backpack down, I took a sip of coffee. When I took a sip, the bus went over a bump in the road, and the coffee spilled on me. I ran to the restroom to clean up before I went to class. Then I ran to class because I was late. When I sat down, I noticed that the room was empty. There was no class that day because my teacher was sick.

2 Read the paragraph again. Underline all the time clauses and circle all the time words. Number the two clauses in the sentences with time clauses. Put a *1* over the event that happened first, a *2* over the event that happened second, and a check (✓) over the events that happened at the same time.

Writing Task

1 *Write* Use the paragraph in the Pre-writing Task to help you write a paragraph about an interesting or unusual story that you or someone you know experienced. What happened first? What happened second? What happened at the same time? Use time clauses beginning with *when*, *before*, and *after*.

2 *Self-Edit* Use the editing tips below to improve your sentences. Make any necessary changes.

1. Did you use time clauses with *when*, *before*, and *after* to show the order of events in a story?
2. Did you use *when* to talk about two events that happened at the same time, *before* to introduce the second event in a sentence, and *after* to introduce the first event in a sentence?
3. Did you use time clauses with main clauses?
4. Did you avoid the mistakes in the Avoid Common Mistakes chart on page 177?

Count and Noncount Nouns
Eating Habits

1 | Grammar in the Real World

A Do you think your diet is healthy? Read the article from a college website. What kinds of food are part of a healthy diet?

Santos Community College

HOME   CONTACT   NEWS   HEALTH

Food for Health

When you turn on a television or read a **newspaper**, you often find **information** about healthy eating. **Food** and **health** get a lot of **attention** in the **news** these **days**. Researchers seem to find new **things** about how our **diet** affects us every day.

5   Everyone knows it is important to eat **fruit** and **vegetables**. Did you know that eating **fruit** and **vegetables** with different colors is especially good for your **health**? Green, red, blue, and orange **fruit** and **vegetables** all have different **vitamins**[1] to help hydrate you, and they help prevent different **diseases**.

Did you know that dark **chocolate** is good for you, too? Research shows that a
10   little **chocolate** helps your **heart** and your **mood**.[2]

How about **fat**?[3] Maybe you think **fat** is bad for you, but people need a little **fat** in their diet. One type of healthy **fat** is omega-3 **oil**.[4] It comes from **fish** and helps your **heart**, **skin**, and **brain** stay healthy. For **vegetarians** or non-fish eaters, many **seeds**[5] and
15   **nuts** also contain omega-3 **oil**. Omega-3 **oil** comes in **pills**, too.

Finally, **water** is an important part of a healthy **diet**. Try to drink at least six **glasses** of **water** a day, and you don't need to buy it. In most places, tap
20   **water** from the kitchen **faucet** is just fine and tastes great!

It is a **challenge** to change your **diet**, but even small **changes** can help you stay healthy and happy.

[1]**vitamin:** a natural substance in food that is important for good health | [2]**mood:** the way someone feels at a particular time | [3]**fat:** a substance in plants and animals, often used for cooking | [4]**omega-3 oil:** a kind of healthy fat | [5]**seed:** a small hard part of a plant from which new plants can grow

B *Comprehension Check* Answer the questions. Use the article to help you.

1. How do colorful fruit and vegetables help your health? *green, red, blue, orange*
2. Why is a little dark chocolate good for you? *It helps our heart and our mood*
3. What type of oil is good for you? *omega-3*
4. How much water is good to drink each day? *6 glasses*

C *Notice* Find the sentences in the web article, and complete them with *a* or *an* or Ø for no article.

1. When you turn on *a* television or read _____*a*_____ newspaper, you often find _____*X*_____ information about healthy eating.

2. _____*X*_____ food and _____*X*_____ health get a lot of attention in the news these days.

3. Maybe you think _____*X*_____ fat is bad for you, but people need a little fat in their diet.

4. It is _____*a*_____ challenge to change your diet, but even small changes can help you stay healthy and happy.

Look at the noun after each space. Which of the nouns are things you can count? Which are things you cannot count?

2 | Count and Noncount Nouns

▶ Grammar Presentation

Nouns are words for people, places, and things.	**Count nouns** name things you can count.
	peas, vegetables, eggs, cookies
There are two types of nouns: count nouns and noncount nouns.	**Noncount nouns** name things you cannot count.
	spinach, water, cheese, sugar

B **Over to You** Complete the lists with words from the chart. Write *count* after count nouns and *noncount* after noncount nouns.

I never eat / drink . . .	I often eat / drink . . .	
apples – count	beef	seafood
beans – count	bread	shrimp
cookies – count	butter	sugar
potatoes – count	cheese	water
sandwiches – count	fish	
tomatoes – count	garlic	
vegetables – count	ice cream	
	meat	
	milk	
	rice	
	salt	

Exercise 2.2 A and *An*

A Complete the survey questions. Write *a* or *an* before the count nouns. Write Ø before noncount nouns.

1. Do you usually have _a_ sandwich for lunch?

2. Do you often have _a_ snack at bedtime?

3. Do you put _×_ salt on your food?

4. Do you eat _×_ garlic before a class?

5. How do you drink your tea or coffee? With _×_ milk and _×_ sugar?

6. Do you usually have _a_ cookie with your tea or coffee?

7. Do you like _×_ butter on your potatoes?

8. How often do you eat _×_ pasta?

9. Which do you prefer: _an_ apple or _a_ banana?

10. Do you prefer _×_ cereal or _×_ bread for breakfast?

B **Pair Work** Ask a partner the survey questions in A.

   A Do you usually have a sandwich for lunch?
   B No, I usually have an omelet or a Caesar salad.

Exercise 2.3 Count and Noncount Nouns

Read about the eating habits of these people. Change the singular count nouns in bold to plural nouns. Write Ø next to the noncount nouns.

Sean

I'm a vegetarian.
1. I don't eat **meat** Ø .
2. I eat **egg**s , but not every day.
3. I also eat **nut** S , and I love fresh **vegetable** S .
4. I also like **apple**S and **cheese** × a lot.

Isabel

I don't like dairy food.
5. I don't eat **cheese** × or **butter** × .
6. I don't drink **milk** × .
7. I love **seafood** × , but I'm allergic to **shrimp** × .
8. My favorite food is **bean** S .
9. I eat a lot of **pasta** × .

Lin

I love fast food.
10. I love potato **chip** S and **cookie** S .
11. I don't eat **vegetable** S very often.
12. I love desserts with **ice cream** × .
13. I'm allergic to **chocolate** × !

Exercise 2.4 Singular and Plural Verbs with Nouns

A Complete the sentences from a magazine article about food. Use the correct form of the verbs in parentheses. *(круглые скобки)*

Food Facts

Food satisfies hunger, but it does other things, too. Food can have good and bad effects on your body and sometimes your mind. Did you know these facts about these common foods?

- Carrots __are__ (be) good for your eyes.
  (1)

- Pasta __makes__ (make) some people sleepy.
  (2)

- Bananas __give__ (give) you energy.
  (3)

- Garlic __is__ (be) good for your heart.
  (4)

- Ice __gives__ (give) some people a headache.
  (5)

- Ice cream __makes__ (make) some people thirsty.
  (6)

- Spinach __contains__ (contain) vitamin C.
  (7)

- Fish __is__ (be) good for your brain.
  (8)

- Some people say green tea __keeps__ (keep) you thin.
  (9)

- Some people say cheese __gives__ (give) them nightmares.
  (10)

- Some people say milk __helps__ (help) them sleep.
  (11)

B *Over to You* Write four sentences about how different kinds of foods affect you.

Ice cream makes me thirsty.
Soda gives me a headache.

1. Chocolate makes me happy.
2. Coffee gives me energy.
3. Bananas give me a stomach-ache.
4. Blueberries are good for my eyes.

3 Units of Measure; *How Many . . . ?* and *How Much . . . ?*

count
noncount

Grammar Presentation

Units of measure help us to tell how much or how many of a noun.	*I bought **a cup of** coffee in the cafeteria.* *We had **a bowl of** soup with lunch.*
Questions with *How much . . . ?* and *How many . . . ?* ask about quantities.	***How many** vegetables did you use?* ***How much** rice do you eat each week?*

3.1 Units of Measure

Unit of Measure	Noncount or Plural Count Noun
a cup of	coffee
a bag of	rice
a piece of	cheese
a bottle of	water
a bowl of	soup
two bags of	potato chips
a carton of	eggs
a bunch of	bananas
a pound of	apples
three boxes of	cookies
a loaf of	bread

⏭ Noncount Nouns and Containers: See page A17.

3.2 Using Units of Measure with Count and Noncount Nouns

a. You can use units of measure to count some noncount nouns.	*My mother gave me **a bottle of** water.* *She drinks **a cup of** coffee every day.* *Did you eat **a piece of** cheese?*
You can make these expressions plural.	*She took **two bottles of** water.* *I drank **three cups of** coffee today.* *We served **some pieces of** cheese.*
b. You can use units of measure with count nouns.	*I bought **a bag of** apples.* *David ate **a box of** cookies!*
You can make these expressions plural.	*We collected **some bags of** apples.* *Lisa sold **six boxes of** cookies.*

pluar

How many+ coun+ noun +...
how much + noncount + noun +...

3.3 *How Many . . . ?* and *How Much . . . ?*

How Many	Count Noun		*How Much*	Noncount Noun	
How many	**apples people bags**	did you eat? want food? do you have?	**How much**	**coffee sugar money**	do you drink every day? do you put in your coffee? do we need?

how much knowledge about cake does Kei have?
how much rice do you eat?

3.4 Using *How Many . . . ?* and *How Much . . . ?*

a. Use *How many . . . ?* to ask about count nouns.	***How many eggs*** *do you eat every week?* ***How many apples*** *do you bring to school every day?*
b. Use *How much . . . ?* to ask about noncount nouns.	***How much milk*** *do you drink a day?* ***How much meat*** *do you eat in a week?*

▶ # Grammar Application

Exercise 3.1 Units of Measure

Complete the menu with the units of measure from the box. You can use some units of measure more than once. Sometimes there is more than one correct answer.

a bag of	a bowl of	a glass of	a plate of
a bottle of	a cup of	a piece of	

Welcome to the Class Picnic!
MENU

Drinks

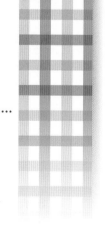

_____*a cup of*_____ coffee or tea
(1)
_____*a bottle of*_____ water or juice
(2)
_____*a glass of*_____ lemonade or iced tea
(3)

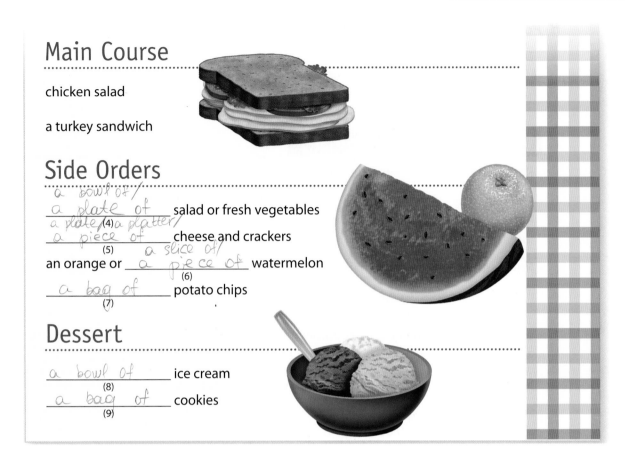

Main Course

chicken salad

a turkey sandwich

Side Orders

a bowl of /
a plate of salad or fresh vegetables
a plate (4) a platter/
a piece of cheese and crackers
(5)
a slice of /
an orange or _a piece of_ watermelon
(6)
a bag of potato chips
(7)

Dessert

a bowl of ice cream
(8)
a bag of cookies
(9)

Exercise 3.2 *How Much . . . ?* and *How Many . . . ?*

A ◀)) Complete each question about the class picnic with *How much* or *How many*.
Then listen to the conversation about the picnic and answer the questions.

1. ___How many___ students are there in the class?   ___18___

2. _____ money do they have?   _____

3. _____ people want water?   _____

4. _____ juice do they need?   _____

5. _____ people want sandwiches?   _____

6. _____ bags of potato chips do they need?   _____

7. _____ salad do they need?   _____

8. _____ cheese do people want?   _____

9. _____ people want an orange?   _____

10. _____ watermelon do they need?   _____

B *Pair Work* Plan a class picnic. Use the menu in Exercise 3.1 and the questions in A to help you.

> *A How many students are there in our group?*
>
> *B There are eight. How many people want water?*

Data from the Real World

Research shows that these are some of the most common noncount nouns:

equipment	homework	love	music	traffic
fun	information	mail	peace	weather
furniture	insurance	money	software	work

Noncount nouns are of the names of:

materials: *oil, plastic, wood*	**Oil** *costs a lot these days.*
groups of things: *money, cash, furniture, jewelry*	*The* **jewelry** *in this store is expensive.*
subjects: *chemistry, geography, psychology*	**Chemistry** *doesn't interest me at all.*
weather: *snow, ice, fog*	*There's always* **snow** *in the winter here.*

Some noncount nouns end in -s, but they take a singular verb:

subjects: *economics, physics, politics*	**Economics** *was my best subject in high school.*
activities: *aerobics, gymnastics*	**Gymnastics** *is my favorite sport.*
other: *news*	*The* **news** *is really good.*

Students often make mistakes with noncount nouns, especially these:

information	equipment	advice	research	knowledge	furniture
behavior	work	homework	software	damage	training

Exercise 3.3 Categories and Items

A Complete the chart. Use the words in the box.

- a check _auleau_
- a couch
- equipment
- an exercise
- furniture
- homework
- information
- jewelry
- a keyboard
- knowledge
- money
- motorcycles
- music
- pop
- rain
- a ring
- traffic _траислор._
- weather

Category: _jewelry_ (1)	Category: _furniture_ (3)	Category: _equipment_ (5)
earrings	a table	a computer
a necklace	a chair	a printer
a ring (2)	_a couch_ (4)	_a keyboard_ (6)
Category: _knowledge_ (7)	Category: _traffic_ (9)	Category: _homework_ (11)
names	cars	an essay
dates	trucks	a reading
information (8)	_motorcycles_ (10)	_an exercise_ (12)
Category: _music_ (13)	Category: _money_ (15)	Category: _weather_ (17)
classical	bills	snow
hip-hop	coins	ice
pop (14)	_a check_ (16)	_rain_ (18)

B *Group Work* Look at the categories in A. How many new words can you add?

4 | Avoid Common Mistakes ⚠

1. **Do not use *a / an* with noncount nouns.**

   I'm doing ⌀ research on eating habits.

2. **Do not make noncount nouns plural or use them with a plural verb.**

   advice
   My teacher gave me some useful ~~advices~~.

3. **Do not use *these* or *those* with noncount nouns.**

   this information is
   I hope ~~these informations are~~ useful.

4. **Use *how much* with noncount nouns, and use *how many* with count nouns.**

   much   *many*
   How ~~many~~ money do you have?   How ~~much~~ classes did you take?

Editing Task

Find and correct the mistakes on this school's website.

Cooking School

LaMoor College *Student Advice Center*

Hotel and Restaurant Program Frequently Asked Questions

1. *Where can I get ~~an~~ information about the study program?*

   Look on the department website for these informations. You can also find an important news on the website and lots of helpful information.

2. *How much classes can I take each semester?*

   Students can take four to six classes each semester.

3. *Is there modern equipments at the college?*

   Yes, our kitchens have brand-new equipment! The college also has new furnitures and computers.

4. *How many homework do professors assign?*

   Every class is different, but professors will always help you if you have a problem with your homeworks.

5. *Does the school give an advice about employment and works?*

   Yes! Our career counselor has knowledges about local employers perfect for you.

---

5 | Grammar for Writing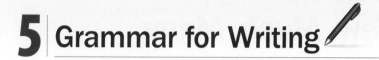

Writing About Meals

Writers use both noncount and count nouns when they write about things such as food. Remember:

- **Use units of measure to show amounts of noncount nouns. Units of measure include count nouns, so you can make them singular or plural.**

	COUNT NOUN	NONCOUNT NOUN
Ignacio used	two pounds of	fish in his fish soup.
I always have	a cup of	strong coffee in the morning.

- **Use singular pronouns to refer to noncount nouns. Use plural or singular pronouns to refer to count nouns.**

  There wasn't very much sugar. _It_ was also very old. (noncount noun)
  The plates are dirty. _They_ are all in the dishwasher. (count noun)

Pre-writing Task

1 Read the paragraph below. How many problems did the writer have with his meal?

A Meal with Friends

Last week I cooked a meal for my friends. The food looked good, but it wasn't very tasty.

First, I served vegetable soup. It looked beautiful, but it tasted like water. Then I served fish. I gave

each person a piece of salmon, but my friends didn't eat very much of it. It was a little dry. We had

mashed potatoes, but they were a little salty. For dessert, I gave everyone a piece of apple pie and

vanilla ice cream. Fortunately, the pie and the ice cream were delicious. My friends were happy

and we had a good time together. I decided to invite my friends for another meal soon.

2 Read the paragraph again. Circle the count nouns and underline the noncount nouns. Double underline the units of measure that go with the noncount nouns.

Writing Task

1 *Write* Use the paragraph in the Pre-writing Task to help you write a paragraph about a meal you cooked or ate recently. What was good? What wasn't good? Describe the food in the meal. Use sentences with units of measure before your noncount nouns.

2 *Self-Edit* Use the editing tips below to improve your sentences. Make any necessary changes.

1. Did you use count and noncount nouns to describe the food?
2. Did you use units of measure to describe the amounts of the noncount food?
3. Did you use the correct pronouns?
4. Did you avoid the mistakes in the Avoid Common Mistakes chart on page 192?

Quantifiers: *Some, Any, A Lot Of, A Little, A Few, Much, Many*

Languages

1 | Grammar in the Real World

A Do you know any words that originally come from another language? Read the blog. What languages do some English words come from?

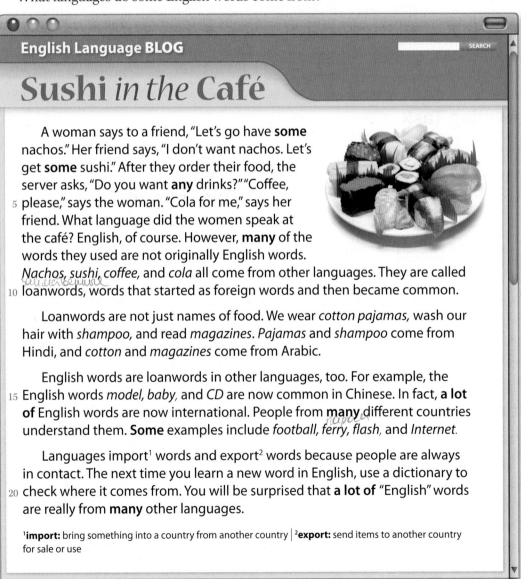

English Language BLOG   SEARCH

Sushi *in the* Café

A woman says to a friend, "Let's go have **some** nachos." Her friend says, "I don't want nachos. Let's get **some** sushi." After they order their food, the server asks, "Do you want **any** drinks?" "Coffee,
5 please," says the woman. "Cola for me," says her friend. What language did the women speak at the café? English, of course. However, **many** of the words they used are not originally English words. *Nachos, sushi, coffee,* and *cola* all come from other languages. They are called
10 loanwords, words that started as foreign words and then became common.

Loanwords are not just names of food. We wear *cotton pajamas,* wash our hair with *shampoo,* and read *magazines. Pajamas* and *shampoo* come from Hindi, and *cotton* and *magazines* come from Arabic.

English words are loanwords in other languages, too. For example, the
15 English words *model, baby,* and *CD* are now common in Chinese. In fact, **a lot of** English words are now international. People from **many** different countries understand them. **Some** examples include *football, ferry, flash,* and *Internet.*

Languages import[1] words and export[2] words because people are always in contact. The next time you learn a new word in English, use a dictionary to
20 check where it comes from. You will be surprised that **a lot of** "English" words are really from **many** other languages.

[1]**import:** bring something into a country from another country │ [2]**export:** send items to another country for sale or use

B Comprehension Check Answer the questions. Use the article to help you.

1. From which language did *pajamas* come? _Hindi_

2. Which English words are commonly used in China? _Model, baby and CD are common in Chinese._

3. Is *football* an original English word? _Yes._

4. Which language did *ferry* come from? _English_

C Notice Find the sentences in the article and complete them with *some* or *any*.

1. Let's go have _Some_ nachos.

2. Let's get _Some_ sushi.

3. The server asks, "Do you want _any_ drinks?"

Compare the sentences with *some* and *any*. How are they different?

2 | Quantifiers: *Some* and *Any*

▶ Grammar Presentation

We use *some* and *any* to talk about an unknown quantity of something.	*Let's go have **some** sushi.* *Do you want **any** drinks?*

* of the noun

2.1 Affirmative Statements with *Some*

	Some	Noncount Noun		Some	Plural Noun
I need		**information.**	Let's have		**nachos.**
Ricardo had	**some**	**sushi.**	I know	**some**	**Italian words.**
We ordered		**food.**	Here are		**examples.**

2.2 Negative Statements with *Any*

	Do/Does/Did + Not	Base Form of Verb	Any	Noncount Noun
I	**don't**	**want**		**sushi.**
The book	**doesn't**	**have**	**any**	**information.**
We	**didn't**	**bring**		**food.**

	Do/Does/Did + Not	Base Form of Verb	Any	Plural Noun
I	**don't**	**remember**		**Italian words.**
Yuri	**doesn't**	**want**	**any**	**nachos.**
We	**didn't**	**see**		**examples.**

HV + S + Base Verb. + ...

2.3 Yes/No Questions with *Some* and *Any*

	Some/Any	Noncount Noun	
Can I have	**some**	**sushi**?	
Do you have	**any**	**information**	about the English program?
Did you do	**any**	**research**	on loanwords?

Some:
- smaller
- specific

Any:
- desperate
- not specific

	Some/Any	Plural Noun	
Can you teach me	**some**	**words**	in Italian?
Do you have	**any**	**books**	on loanwords?
Are there	**any**	**examples**	in the book?

2.4 Using *Some* and *Any* in Statements

a. Use *some* with noncount nouns and plural nouns in affirmative statements.	I found **some information** about loanwords in this book.
In affirmative statements *some* refers to small quantities or unknown quantities.	There are **some words** in English that come from Arabic, but I don't know how many.
b. Use *some* for small amounts and numbers, not large amounts and numbers.	There are Latin and Greek words in English. NOT ~~There are **some** Latin and Greek words in English.~~ (There are thousands!)
c. Use *any* with noncount nouns and plural nouns in negative statements.	There isn't **any food** in the refrigerator.
In negative statements *any* refers to a zero quantity.	I don't remember **any words** in Italian.

Some
- small amounts
- unknown amounts
- small numbers

Any
(negative)
- "zero amout" (none)

2.5 Using Yes/No Questions with *Some* and *Any*

a. Use *some* with noncount nouns and plural nouns to ask for something or to offer something that is there.	Can I get **some** information from you about Portuguese, please? (The person asking knows the other person has information about Portuguese.) Do you want to use **some** words from Russian for your paper about English loanwords? (The person asking has words to give to the writer.)
b. Use *any* with noncount nouns and plural nouns to ask for unknown quantities.	Did you make **any** progress with your paper? (The questioner doesn't expect progress.) Are there **any** English words that come from Swahili? (There may be no English words that come from Swahili. The questioner doesn't know.)

Yes/No
- No "Wh"
- Starts with helping verb

196 Unit 17 Quantifiers: *Some, Any, A Lot Of, A Little, A Few, Much, Many*

3.3 Using Quantifiers

a. In affirmative statements:	
Use *a lot of* for large quantities of plural nouns and noncount nouns.	*I met **a lot of** Russian speakers in North Carolina. There is **a lot of** help available for students.*
Use *a little* for small quantities of noncount nouns.	*I understand **a little** Swedish.*
Use *a few* for small quantities of plural nouns.	*Dane has **a few** friends in Asia.*
Use *many* for large quantities of plural nouns.	*There are **many** people that speak Swahili in the neighborhood.*
b. In negative statements:	
Use *not a lot of* for small amounts of plural and noncount nouns.	*There is**n't a lot of** information about some words. There are**n't a lot of** students from Denmark at the school.*
Use *not much* for small amounts of noncount nouns.	*Two months is**n't much** time to learn a new language.*
Use *not many* for small amounts of plural nouns.	*There are**n't many** people from Austria in my class.*
c. In questions:	
Use *a lot of* with plural and noncount nouns.	*Do you have **a lot of** relatives in Ireland? Is there **a lot of** bad weather in Maine?*
Use *much* in questions with noncount nouns.	*Do you have **much** homework in Spanish class?*
Use *many* with plural nouns.	*Are there **many** Chinese restaurants in Boston?*
d. Don't use *much* in affirmative statements.	*The website had **a lot of** information about Latin.* NOT *~~The website had much information about Latin.~~*
e. Use short answers with *a lot, a few,* and *not many* to refer to plural nouns.	*"How **many** students did a presentation on loanwords?" "**A lot. / A few. / Not many.**"*
Use short answers with *a lot, a little,* and *not much* to refer to noncount nouns.	*"How **much** work did you do on your paper?" "**A lot. / A little. / Not much.**"*

▶ Grammar Application

Exercise 3.1 Count and Noncount Nouns

Write *C* for the count nouns and *NC* for the noncount nouns.

dictionary _C_   homework _____   student _____   song _____   furniture _____

time _____   music _____   knowledge _____   word _____   Korean (language) _____

Exercise 3.2 *A Lot Of*, *A Little*, *A Few*, or *Many*

◀))) Listen and complete the paragraph about an English class with *a lot of*, *a little*, *a few*, or *many*.

Karina's English class at Dixon College is very international. Her class has _a few_ Russians: Karina and two others.
(1)

There are _____ students
(2)
from Brazil, perhaps 80 percent. There are

_____ students from Japan,
(3)
but not many. The rest are from other Asian countries like Malaysia, Thailand, and Vietnam.

They come from all over the world and bring interesting stories with them. Rosa is from São Paulo, Brazil, and listens to _____ Brazilian music. She loves it.
(4)

She also has _____ songs from Puerto Rico on her computer, but not many.
(5)

Seri, from Penang, has _____ beautiful furniture from Malaysia in her house.
(6)

Keiko, from Japan, taught Karina and Rosa _____ Japanese, but the words are
(7)

difficult to remember. Noom, from Bangkok, loves his country's food. Sometimes he makes

_____ Thai food for his classmates, but not much because it's very hot for
(8)

them. Linh, who moved from Vietnam, eats _____ spicy food. She loves it!
(9)

Sometimes, Karina brings in _____ *borscht*, a Russian soup. Only Keiko and
(10)

Noom like it, so she doesn't make a lot of it. The best part of Karina's diverse class is that she

can hear _____ languages besides English every day!
(11)

Exercise 3.3 *A Lot Of, A Little, A Few, Much*, or *Many*

A Circle the correct words.

Dustin   Hi, Dr. Lanza. Thank you for doing this interview

for *Student Voices*. First, are there **much / (many)**
(1)

countries in Asia where English is the official

language?

Dr. Lanza   Well, there aren't **many / much**, but there are
(2)

a little / a few – for example, Pakistan, Singapore,
(3)

and the Philippines.

Dustin   How **many / much** words are there in English?
(4)

Dr. Lanza   It's hard to say. Anywhere from 250,000 to 750,000, perhaps! Dictionaries

have **much / a lot of** words, but they don't contain all of them. A big
(5)

English dictionary has hundreds of thousands of words.

Dustin   Really? That's **many / a lot**! How many words do native English speakers
(6)

know? Do they know **a lot of / many** vocabulary?
(7)

Dr. Lanza   Yes, every native speaker knows **much / a lot of** words. Adults probably
(8)

know 20,000 to 30,000 words.

Dustin   Very interesting! Thanks for this interview, Dr. Lanza!

B *Pair Work*   Tell a partner what you know about other cultures and languages. Use the
conversation in A as a model. Remember to use *a lot of, a few, a little,* and *many*.

Exercise 3.4 Short Answers

Answer the questions that students in an English class are asking each other before class. Use *a lot, a few, a little, not many,* and *not much.*

1. How much time did you work on your paper?

   _A lot_____. I worked all day on it.

2. I wasn't in class yesterday. How much homework did we have for today?

   _____. The teacher only assigned two exercises in our Workbook.

3. How many classes do you have today?

   _____. I only have two today. Tomorrow I have four!

4. How much time did you spend on homework last night?

   _____. I was very busy, so I didn't have a lot of time.

5. How many minutes do we have before class starts?

   _____. It's going to start in two minutes!

Exercise 3.5 *A Lot Of*, *Much*, and *Many*

Data from the Real World

People often use *a lot of* in speaking. In writing, they often use *much* and *many*.	Say: "There are a lot of different languages and cultures in South America." Write: There are many different languages and cultures in South America. Say: "Schools in poorer countries often don't have a lot of modern equipment." Write: Schools in poorer countries often do not have much modern equipment.	**a lot of** writing speaking
Use *a lot of* in speaking and writing in affirmative statements with noncount nouns.	*The website has a lot of information about English as a global language.*	

A Change *a lot of* to *much* or *many* in the essay.

Communication Shortage?

many

In the twentieth century, ~~a lot of~~ young people had pen pals[1] from other countries. They wrote letters to them and learned about other countries, cultures, and languages. Traveling was expensive, so they did not have **a lot of** opportunities to meet their pen pals. There was not **a lot**

5 **of** direct contact between people from different countries, so letters were a good way to communicate.

Now there are not **a lot of** traditional pen pals. Instead, there are **a lot of** social networking sites on the Internet. People can send electronic messages across the world from these sites. Most young people are very

10 busy and do not have **a lot of** time to write long messages, so messages are short. Today, friends typically send **a lot of** messages, one after another. However, can people exchange **a lot of** information in very short online messages? Can people learn **a lot of** interesting things about the other person's culture in these short messages? This is a good question

15 for discussion.

[1]**pen pal:** someone you exchange letters with as a hobby, especially someone from another country

B *Pair Work* Discuss the essay in A with a partner. Ask each other these questions.

1. Do you have friends you communicate with electronically?
2. Do you think social networking sites are a good way to learn about other countries and cultures? Can you learn a lot from them?
3. What kinds of information do people exchange on social networking sites?

4 Avoid Common Mistakes ⚠

1. Use *many* with plural nouns.

    many
Do you write ~~much~~ essays?

2. Use *much* with noncount nouns in <u>negative</u> statements and questions. In affirmative statements with noncount nouns, use *a lot of*, not *much*.

           much
The students don't have ~~many~~ work in the lab today.
   a lot of
There is ~~much~~ information on loanwords online.

3. For quantities, use *some* with noncount nouns. Do not use *a / an* with noncount nouns.

   some
I need ~~an~~ information about Korea.

4. Use *any* with negative statements, and use *some* with affirmative statements.

        any   *some*
I don't have ~~some~~ dictionaries to use.   I learned ~~any~~ Japanese words from a Japanese friend.

Editing Task

Find and correct 11 more mistakes in this interview with Dr. Matthew Sutton, Director of the Language Center at Marsland College.

Roberto Hello, Dr. Sutton. My name is Roberto
Ferrer and I'm a student here at the
                       some
college. I'd like to ask you ~~any~~ questions
about the Language Center for our
5   college paper. How does the Language
Center help language students?

Dr. Sutton Thanks for asking, Roberto. The center
is very important. We give students
much information about foreign
10   languages and cultures, and we have much learning material for 30
different languages.

Roberto Wow, that sounds like much information on different languages that
students can find here.

Dr. Sutton It is, Roberto. Much students find the center really helpful. You see,

15 much students work and do not have many time to study. They can

come to the center before or after class. They can spend a few minutes

or one or two hours here. They can do any exercises, or use our CDs and

DVDs, or read, or just meet friends.

Roberto That sounds great. Do much students use the center?

20 *Dr. Sutton* Right now, about 100 students use the center every day.

Roberto Does the center have modern equipment?

Dr. Sutton Yes, it does. Every year, we buy a new equipment, for example,

computers and DVD players. We also spend much money to make the

center a comfortable place. For example, we recently bought a new

25 furniture. Please come and visit! We are open every day.

Roberto All right. Thanks for your time, Dr. Sutton!

5 | Grammar for Writing ✏

Writing About Indefinite Quantities of Things

Writers use the quantifiers *some, any, a lot of, a little, a few, much*, and *many* with nouns when they write about indefinite amounts of things.

Remember:

- **Use *a lot of, much*, and *many* to talk about big quantities, and use *a little* and *a few* to talk about small quantities.**

  Gabe knows <u>a lot of</u> Spanish, but he knows only <u>a little</u> Portuguese.

  Nimita cooks <u>many</u> Indian dishes, but she cooks only <u>a few</u> Mexican dishes.

- **Use *some* to write about plural count and noncount nouns when the exact amount of the noun isn't important or isn't known. Use *not any* when there is none of a plural count or noncount noun.**

  Soraida plays <u>some</u> great Mexican songs on the guitar. She does <u>not</u> play <u>any</u> Mexican songs on the piano.

Pre-writing Task

1 Read the paragraph below. What types of English loanwords does Arabic use, and which Arabic loanwords does the writer write about?

English and Arabic Loanwords

I am from Oman. In Oman we speak Arabic. We have (a lot of) English words in our language. Classical Arabic does not have any English loanwords, but modern Arabic has a lot. We use <u>a few</u> clothing words. For example, we say *jeans, jacket,* and *T-shirt*. We also use many English computer words, such as *format, save,* and *file*. There are a few English words for food in our language, such as *hot dog, hamburger,* and *ice cream*. A lot of young people use the word *cool*. There are many Arabic words in other languages, too. Some Arabic words in English are *coffee* and *sofa*. Not many people know that these words originally came from Arabic.

2 Read the paragraph again. Circle the quantifiers for big quantities of things and underline the quantifiers for small quantities of things.

Writing Task

1 *Write* Use the paragraph in the Pre-writing Task to help you write a paragraph about something that you have or use that comes from a different country or culture. Write about the amount of this thing in your culture. Is there some of it, a lot of it, or a little of it? You can write about:

- cars
- clothing
- food
- jewelry
- music
- restaurants
- tourists
- words
- your ideas

Use sentences with quantifiers such as:

- We use a lot of _____.
- We don't have much _____.
- They have some _____.
- They don't have any _____.

2 *Self-Edit* Use the editing tips below to improve your sentences. Make any necessary changes.

1. Did you use indefinite quantifiers to write about things in your culture or from another culture?
2. Did you use *a lot of*, *much*, and *many* to talk about big quantities, and *a little* and *a few* to talk about small quantities?
3. Did you use *some* to write about unknown or unimportant amounts, and *not any* to write about nouns that there are none of?
4. Did you avoid the mistakes in the Avoid Common Mistakes chart on page 206?

Appendices

1. Capitalization and Punctuation Rules

Capitalize	Examples
1. The first letter of the first word of a sentence	*Today is a great day.*
2. The pronoun *I*	*Yesterday I went to hear a new rock band.*
3. Names of people	*Simón Bolívar, Joseph Chung*
4. Names of buildings, streets, geographic locations, and organizations	*Taj Majal, Broadway, Mt. Everest, United Nations*
5. Titles of people	*Dr., Mr., Mrs., Ms.*
6. Days, months, and holidays	*Tuesday, April, Valentine's Day*
7. Names of courses or classes	*Biology 101, English Composition II*
8. Titles of books, movies, and plays	*Crime and Punishment, Avatar, Hamlet*
9. States, countries, languages, and nationalities	*California, Mexico, Spanish, South Korean, Canadian*
10. Names of religions	*Hinduism, Catholicism, Islam, Judaism*

Punctuation	Examples
1. Use a period (.) at the end of a sentence.	*He is Korean.*
2. Use a question mark (?) at the end of a question.	*Do you want to buy a car?*
3. Use an exclamation point (!) to show strong emotion (e.g., surprise, anger, shock).	*Wait! I'm not ready yet. I can't believe it!*

4. Use an apostrophe (') for possessive nouns.
    Add *'s* for singular nouns.
    Add *s'* for plural nouns.
    Add *'s* for irregular plural nouns.
Use an apostrophe (') for contractions.
	That's Sue's umbrella.
	Those are the students' books. BUT
	Bring me the children's shoes.
	I'll be back next week. He can't drive a car.

5. Use a comma (,): • between words in a series of three or more items. (Place *and* before the last item.) • before *and, or, but,* and *so* to connect two complete sentences.	*I like fish, chicken, turkey, and mashed potatoes.* *You can watch TV, but I have to study for a test.*

2. Spelling Rules for Noun Plurals

1. Add *-s* to most singular nouns to form plural nouns.	*a camera – two cameras* *a key – keys*	*a model – two models* *a student – students*
2. Add *-es* to nouns that end in *-ch, -sh, -ss,* and *-x*.	*watch – watches* *class – classes*	*dish – dishes* *tax – taxes*
3. With nouns that end in a consonant + *-y,* change the *y* to *i* and add *-es*.	*accessory – accessories*	*battery – batteries*
4. With nouns that end in *-ife,* change the ending to *-ives*.	*knife – knives* *wife – wives*	*life – lives*
5. Add *-es* to nouns that end in *-o* after a consonant. **Exception:** Add *-s* only to nouns that end in *-o* and refer to music.	*potato – potatoes* *piano – pianos*	*tomato – tomatoes* *soprano – sopranos*
6. Add *-s* to nouns that end in *-o* after a vowel.	*radio – radios*	*shampoo – shampoos*
7. Some plural nouns have irregular forms. These are the most common irregular plural nouns in academic writing.	*man – men* *child – children* *foot – feet*	*woman – women* *person – people* *tooth – teeth*
8. Some nouns have the same form for singular and plural.	*one deer – two deer* *one fish – two fish*	*one sheep – two sheep*
9. Some nouns are only plural. They do not have a singular form.	*clothes* *glasses* *headphones* *jeans*	*pants* *scissors* *sunglasses*

3. Verb Forms

Present: Be
Affirmative Statements

SINGULAR			
Subject	*Be*		
I	**am**		
You	**are**	late.	
He She It	**is**		
		difficult.	

PLURAL		
Subject	*Be*	
We You They	**are**	from Seoul.

Negative Statements

SINGULAR		
Subject	*Be + Not*	
I	**am not**	
You	**are not**	in class.
He She It	**is not**	

PLURAL		
Subject	*Be + Not*	
We You They	**are not**	students.

Affirmative Contractions

SINGULAR		
I am	→	I**'m**
You are	→	You**'re**
He is	→	He**'s**
Jun-Ho is	→	Jun-Ho**'s**
She is	→	She**'s**
His mother is	→	His mother**'s**
It is	→	It**'s**
My name is	→	My name**'s**

PLURAL		
We are	→	We**'re**
You are	→	You**'re**
They are	→	They**'re**

Negative Contractions

SINGULAR		
I am not	→	I**'m not**
You are not	→	You**'re not** / You **aren't**
He is not	→	He**'s not** / He **isn't**
She is not	→	She**'s not** / She **isn't**
It is not	→	It**'s not** / It **isn't**

PLURAL		
We are not	→	We**'re not** / We **aren't**
You are not	→	You**'re not** / You **aren't**
They are not	→	They**'re not** / They **aren't**

Singular Yes/No Questions

Be	Subject	
Am	I	
Are	you	in class?
Is	he she it	

Singular Short Answers

AFFIRMATIVE		
	Subject	Be
Yes,	I	**am**.
	you	**are**.
	he she it	**is**.

NEGATIVE		
	Subject	Be + Not
No,	I	**am not**.
	you	**are not**.
	he she it	**is not**.

Plural Yes/No Questions

Be	Subject	
Are	we you they	late?

Plural Short Answers

AFFIRMATIVE		
	Subject	Be
Yes,	we you they	**are**.

NEGATIVE		
	Subject	Be + Not
No,	we you they	**are not**.

Negative Short Answer Contractions

SINGULAR		
No, I am not.	→	No, I**'m not**.
No, you are not.	→	No, you**'re not**. No, you **aren't**.
No, he is not.	→	No, he**'s not**. No, he **isn't**.
No, she is not.	→	No, she**'s not**. No, she **isn't**.
No, it is not.	→	No, it**'s not**. No, it **isn't**.

PLURAL		
No, we are not.	→	No, we**'re not**. No, we **aren't**.
No, you are not.	→	No, you**'re not**. No, you **aren't**.
No, they are not.	→	No, they**'re not**. No, they **aren't**.

Information Questions

SINGULAR SUBJECTS				PLURAL SUBJECTS		
Wh- Word	*Be*	Subject		*Wh-* Word	*Be*	Subject
Who		your teacher?		**Who**		your teachers?
What		your major?		**What**		your plans?
When	is	our exam?		**When**	are	your exams?
Where		the building?		**Where**		your books?
How		your class?		**How**		your classes?

Contractions with Singular Subjects

Who is	→	**Who's**
What is	→	**What's**
When is	→	**When's**
Where is	→	**Where's**
How is	→	**How's**

There Is / There Are

Affirmative Statements

There	Be	Subject	Place/Time
There	**is**	a parking lot a free tour	on Alameda Street. at 10:00.
	are	a lot of little shops free tours	in the area. on most days.

Contraction
There is → There's

Negative Statements

There	Be + Not/No	Subject	Place/Time
There	**isn't** **is no**	a bank bank	in Union Station.
	isn't **is no**	a show show	at 8:00.
There	**'s no**	bank	in Union Station.
		show	at 8:00.
There	**aren't** **are no**	any cars cars	on Olvera Street.
	aren't **are no**	any tours tours	in the evening.

Yes/No Questions and Short Answers

Be	There	Subject	Place/Time
Is	**there**	a visitor's center	on Olvera Street?
		a performance	at 6:00?
Are		any parking lots	in the area?
		any tours	in the evening?

Short Answers
Yes, **there is**.
No, **there isn't**.
Yes, **there are**.
No, **there aren't**.

Simple Present

Affirmative Statements

SINGULAR			PLURAL		
Subject	**Verb**		**Subject**	**Verb**	
I You	**eat**	vegetables every day.	We You They	**have**	many friends.
He She It	**eats**				

Negative Statements

SINGULAR				PLURAL			
Subject	*Do / Does* + *Not*	**Base Form of Verb**		**Subject**	*Do* + *Not*	**Base Form of Verb**	
I You	**do not** **don't**	**eat**	a lot of meat.	We You They	**do not** **don't**	**exercise**	in the morning.
He She It	**does not** **doesn't**						

Yes / No Questions

Do / Does	**Subject**	**Base Form of Verb**	
Do	I you we they	**fall asleep**	in 30 minutes?
Does	he she it		

Short Answers

AFFIRMATIVE			NEGATIVE		
Yes	**Subject**	*Do/Does*	*No*	**Subject**	*Do/Does* + *Not*
Yes,	I you we they	**do**.	No,	I you we they	**do not**. **don't**.
	he she it	**does**.		he she it	**does not**. **doesn't**.

Information Questions

Wh- word	Do / Does	Subject	Base Form of Verb	
Who		I	see	at school?
What	do	you we they	eat	at parties?
When			celebrate	that holiday?
Where		he she it	study	for school?
Why	does		live	at home?
How			meet	new people?

Present Progressive

Affirmative Statements

Subject	Be	Verb + -ing
I	am	
You We They	are	talking.
He She It	is	

Contractions

I am → I'm
You are → You're
We are → We're
They are → They're
He is → He's
She is → She's
It is → It's

Negative Statements

Subject	Be + Not	Verb + -ing
I	am not	
You We They	are not	talking.
He She It	is not	

Contractions

I am not	→ I'm not	
You are not	→ You're not	You aren't
We are not	→ We're not	We aren't
They are not	→ They're not	They aren't
He is not	→ He's not	He isn't
She is not	→ She's not	She isn't
It is not	→ It's not	It isn't

Yes / No Questions

Be	Subject	Verb + -ing
Am	I	
Are	you we they	**working**?
Is	he she it	

Short Answers

AFFIRMATIVE	NEGATIVE	
Yes, I **am**.	No, I**'m not**.	
Yes, you **are**.	No, you**'re not**.	No, you **aren't**.
Yes, we **are**.	No, we**'re not**.	No, we **aren't**.
Yes, they **are**.	No, they**'re not**.	No, they **aren't**.
Yes, he **is**.	No, he**'s not**.	No, he **isn't**.
Yes, she **is**.	No, she**'s not**.	No, she **isn't**.
Yes, it **is**.	No, it**'s not**.	No, it **isn't**.

Information Questions

Wh- Word	Be	Subject	Verb + -ing
Who	am	I	**hearing**?
What		you we they	**studying**?
When	are		**leaving**?
Where			**going**?
Why	is	he she it	**laughing**?
How			**feeling**?

Wh- Word as Subject	Be	Verb + -ing
Who	is	**talking**?
What		**happening**?

Simple Past: *Be*

Statements

AFFIRMATIVE		
Subject	*Was / Were*	
I He She It	**was**	in the computer lab.
We You They	**were**	

NEGATIVE		
Subject	*Was / Were + Not*	
I He She It	**was not** **wasn't**	in class.
We You They	**were not** **weren't**	

Yes / No Questions

Was / Were	Subject	
Was	I he she it	very smart?
Were	we you they	in college?

Short Answers

AFFIRMATIVE			
	Yes	Subject	*Was / Were*
	Yes,	I he she it	**was.**
		we you they	**were.**

NEGATIVE			
	No	Subject	*Was / Were + Not*
	No,	I he she it	**was not.** **wasn't.**
		we you they	**were not.** **weren't.**

Information Questions

Wh- Word	*Was / Were*	Subject	
Who	**was**	your best friend	as a child?
What		your favorite class	last semester?
When		her birthday party?	
What time		the meeting	on Monday?
Where		his partners?	
Why	**were**	they	successful?
How		the concerts	the other night?
How old		their cars	in 2011?

Simple Past

Statements

AFFIRMATIVE		
Subject	Simple Past Verb	
I You We They He She It	**started**	in 1962.

NEGATIVE		
Subject	*Did + Not*	Base Form of Verb	
I You We They He She It	**did not** **didn't**	**sign**	a contract.

Yes / No Questions

Did	Subject	Base Form of Verb	
Did	I you we they he she it	**finish**	the report?

Short Answers

AFFIRMATIVE		
Yes	Subject	*Did*
Yes,	I you we they he she it	**did**.

NEGATIVE		
No	Subject	*Did + Not*
No,	I you we they he she it	**did not**. **didn't**.

Information Questions

Wh- Word	*Did*	Subject	Base Form of Verb	
Who			**write**	about?
What		I you we they he she it	**do**	yesterday?
When	**did**		**finish**	our report?
Where			**visit**	on vacation?
Why			**start**	a company?
How			**save**	enough money?

Past Progressive

Statements

AFFIRMATIVE				NEGATIVE		
Subject	**Past of *Be***	**Verb + *-ing***		**Subject**	**Past of *Be* + *Not***	**Verb + *-ing***
I He She It	**was**			I He She It	**was not / wasn't**	
You We They	**were**	**working**.		You We They	**were not / weren't**	**working**.

Yes / No Questions

Past of *Be*	Subject	Verb + *-ing*
Was	I he she it	**working**?
Were	you we they	**working**?

Short Answers

AFFIRMATIVE				NEGATIVE		
	Subject	**Past of *Be***			**Subject**	**Past of *Be* + *Not***
Yes,	I he she it	**was**.		No,	I he she it	**was not. wasn't**.
	you we they	**were**.			you we they	**were not. weren't**.

Information Questions

Wh- Word	Past of *Be*	Subject	Verb + *-ing*
Who	**was**	I he she it	**studying**?
What			**doing**?
When			**researching**?
Where	**were**	you we they	**working**?
Why			**experimenting**?
How			**feeling**?

Wh- Word as Subject	Past of *Be*	Verb + *-ing*
Who	**was**	**talking**?
What	**was**	**happening**?

Future: *Be Going To*

Statements

AFFIRMATIVE				
Subject	*Be*	*Going To*	Base Form of Verb	
I	**am**			
You We They	**are**	**going to**	get	a job.
He She It	**is**			

NEGATIVE				
Subject	*Be + Not*	*Going To*	Base Form of Verb	
I	**am not**			
You We They	**are not**	**going to**	get	a job.
He She It	**is not**			

Yes / No Questions

Be	Subject	*Going To*	Base Form of Verb	
Am	I			
Are	you we they	**going to**	get	a job?
Is	he she it			

Short Answers

AFFIRMATIVE		
	Subject	*Be*
Yes,	I	**am.**
	you we they	**are.**
	he she it	**is.**

NEGATIVE		
	Subject	*Be + Not*
No,	I	**'m not.**
	you we they	**aren't.**
	he she it	**isn't.**

Information Questions

Wh- Word	*Be*	Subject	*Going To*	Base Form of Verb	
Who	am	I		interview	tomorrow?
What		you we they		do	after graduation?
When	are			leave	for New York?
Where			**going to**	work	after college?
Why	is	he she it		move	to Canada?
How				pay	his loans?

Information Questions

Wh- Word as Subject	Be	Going To	Base Form of Verb	
Who	is	going to	get	a job after college?
What			happen	after school?

Future: *Will*

Statements

AFFIRMATIVE					NEGATIVE				
Subject	Will	Base Form of Verb			Subject	Will + Not	Base Form of Verb		
I You We They He She It	will 'll	have	a healthy life.		I You We They He She It	will not won't	have	a healthy life.	

Yes / No Questions

Will	Subject	Base Form of Verb	
Will	I you we they he she it	have	a healthy life?

Short Answers

AFFIRMATIVE			NEGATIVE	
Yes, I Yes, you Yes, we Yes, they Yes, he Yes, she Yes, it	will.		No, I No, you No, we No, they No, he No, she No, it	won't.

Information Questions

Wh- Word	Will	Subject	Base Form of Verb	
Who		I you we they he she it	meet	at the interview tomorrow?
What			do	in your training program?
When	will		return	your documents?
Where			find	information about careers?
Why			travel	to South America?
How			build	new apartments?

Imperatives

Statements

AFFIRMATIVE			NEGATIVE		
Base Form of Verb			*Do + Not*	Base Form of Verb	
Smile	and be helpful.		Don't / Do not	**interrupt**	people who are very busy.
Look	at people when you talk to them.			**do**	this in the beginning.

4. Common Regular and Irregular Verbs

Regular

Base Form	Past Form
call	called
decide	decided
happen	happened
like	liked
live	lived
look	looked
move	moved
start	started
talk	talked
try	tried
work	worked

Irregular

Base Form	Past Form
come	came
do	did
get	got
go	went
have	had
make	made
put	put
read	read
say	said
see	saw

11. Spelling Rules for Verbs Ending in *-ing*

1. For most verbs, add *-ing**.

go → going   say → saying   talk → talking

2. If the verb ends in a silent *-e*, delete *e* and add *-ing*.

live → living   make → making   write → writing

3. For *be* and *see*, don't drop the *e* because it is not silent.

be → being   see → seeing

4. If the verb ends in *-ie*, change the *ie* to *y* and add *-ing*.

die → dying   lie → lying

5. If the verb has one syllable and follows the pattern consonant, vowel, consonant (CVC), double the last letter and add *-ing*.

get → getting   put → putting   sit → sitting

6. Do not double the consonant if the verb ends in *-w, -x*, or *-y*.

grow → growing   fix → fixing   say → saying

7. If the verb has two syllables, ends in the pattern CVC, and is stressed on the last syllable, double the last letter and add *-ing*.

beGIN → begin**n**ing

8. If the verb has two syllables and is stressed on the first syllable, do not double the last letter.

LISten → listening   TRAVel → traveling   VISit → visiting

* Verbs that end in *-ing* are also called *gerunds* when they are used as a noun. The same spelling rules above apply to gerunds as well.

12. Spelling and Pronunciation Rules for Simple Present

Spelling of Third-Person Singular Verbs

1. Add *-s* to most verbs.
Add *-s* to verbs ending in a vowel* + *-y*.
drink**s**, ride**s**, run**s**, see**s**, sleep**s**   buy**s**, pay**s**, say**s**

2. Add *-es* to verbs ending in *-ch, -sh, -ss, -x*.
Add *-es* to verbs ending in a consonant** + *-o*.
teach**es**, push**es**, miss**es**, fix**es**   do**es**, go**es**

3. For verbs that end in a consonant + *-y*, change the *y* to *i* and add *-es*.
cry → cr**ies**   study → stud**ies**

4. Some verbs are irregular.
be → am / are / is   have → has

* **Vowels:** the letters *a, e, i, o, u*
** **Consonants:** the letters *b, c, d, f, g, h, j, k, l, m, n, p, q, r, s, t, v, w, x, y, z*

Pronunciation of Third-Person Singular Verbs

1. Say /s/ after /f/, /k/, /p/, and /t/ sounds.
laughs, drinks, walks, sleeps, writes, gets

2. Say /z/ after /b/, /d/, /g/, /v/, /m/, /n/, /l/, and /r/ sounds and all vowel sounds.
grabs, rides, hugs, lives, comes, runs, smiles, hears, sees, plays, buys, goes, studies

3. Say /əz/ after /tʃ/, /ʃ/, /s/, /ks/, /z/, and /dʒ/ sounds.
teaches, pushes, kisses, fixes, uses, changes

4. Pronounce the vowel sound in *does* and *says* differently from *do* and *say*.
do /du:/ → *does* /dʌz/
say /seɪ/ → *says* /sez/

13. Spelling and Pronunciation Rules for Regular Verbs in Simple Past

Spelling of Regular Verbs

1. For most verbs, add *-ed*.	*work* → *worked*
2. For verbs ending in *-e*, add *-d*.	*live* → *lived*
3. For verbs ending in consonant + *-y*, change the *y* to *i* and add *-ed*.	*study* → *studied*
4. For verbs ending in vowel + *-y*, add *-ed*.	*play* → *played*
5. For one-syllable verbs ending in consonant-vowel-consonant (CVC), double the consonant.	*plan* → *planned*
6. Do not double the consonant if the verb ends in *-x* or *-w*.	*show* → *showed*
7. For two-syllable verbs ending in CVC and stressed on the first syllable, do not double the consonant.	*TRAvel* → *TRAveled*
8. For two-syllable verbs ending in CVC and stressed on the second syllable, double the consonant.	*conTROL* → *conTROLLED*

Pronunciation of Regular Verbs

1. When the verb ends in /t/ or /d/, say *-ed* as /ɪd/ or /əd/.	*wait* → *waited*	*decide* → *decided*
2. When the verb ends in /f/, /k/, /p/, /s/, /ʃ/, and /tʃ/, say *-ed* as /t/.	*laugh* → *laughed* *look* → *looked* *stop* → *stopped*	*miss* → *missed* *finish* → *finished* *watch* → *watched*
3. For verbs that end in other consonant and vowel sounds, say *-ed* as /d/.	*agree* → *agreed* *borrow* → *borrowed* *change* → *changed*	*listen* → *listened* *live* → *lived* *play* → *played*

14. Adjectives and Adverbs: Comparative and Superlative Forms

		Adjective	Comparative	Superlative
1.	**One-Syllable Adjectives**			
	a. Add *-er* and *-est* to one-syllable adjectives.	cheap	cheaper	the cheapest
		new	newer	the newest
		old	older	the oldest
		small	smaller	the smallest
		strong	stronger	the strongest
		tall	taller	the tallest
		young	younger	the youngest
	b. If the adjective ends with one vowel + one consonant, double the last letter and add *-er* or *-est*. Do not double the consonant *w*.	big	bigger	the biggest
		hot	hotter	the hottest
		sad	sadder	the saddest
		thin	thinner	the thinnest
2.	**Two-Syllable Adjectives**			
	a. Add *more* or *the most* to most two-syllable adjectives.	boring	more boring	the most boring
		famous	more famous	the most famous
		handsome	more handsome	the most handsome
		patient	more patient	the most patient
	b. Some two-syllable adjectives have two forms.	narrow	narrower / more narrow	the narrowest / the most narrow
		simple	simpler / more simple	the simplest / the most simple
	c. If the adjective has two syllables and ends in *-y*, change the *y* to *i* and add *-er* or *-est*.	angry	angrier	the angriest
		easy	easier	the easiest
		friendly	friendlier	the friendliest
		happy	happier	the happiest
		lucky	luckier	the luckiest
		pretty	prettier	the prettiest
		silly	sillier	the silliest

Adjectives and Adverbs: Comparative and Superlative Forms *(continued)*

	Adjective	Comparative	Superlative
3. Three-or-More-Syllable Adjectives Add *more* or *the most* to adjectives with three or more syllables.	beautiful difficult enjoyable expensive important serious	more beautiful more difficult more enjoyable more expensive more important more serious	the most beautiful the most difficult the most enjoyable the most expensive the most important the most serious
4. Irregular Adjectives Some adjectives have irregular forms.	bad far good	worse farther / further better	the worst the farthest / the furthest the best

	Adverb	Comparative	Superlative
1. -ly Adverbs Most adverbs end in *-ly*.	patiently quickly quietly slowly	more patiently more quickly more quietly more slowly	(the) most patiently (the) most quickly (the) most quietly (the) most slowly
2. One-Syllable Adverbs A few adverbs do not end in *-ly*. Add *-er* and *-est* to these adverbs.	fast hard	faster harder	(the) fastest (the) hardest
3. Irregular Adverbs Some adverbs have irregular forms.	badly far well	worse farther / further better	(the) worst (the) farthest / furthest (the) best

People usually only use *the* with superlative adverbs in formal writing and speaking.

15. Adverbs with -ly

Adjective	Adverb	Adjective	Adverb
bad	badly	loud	loudly
beautiful	beautifully	nervous	nervously
careful	carefully	nice	nicely
clear	clearly	patient	patiently
close	closely	polite	politely
confident	confidently	proper	properly
deep	deeply	quick	quickly
fluent	fluently	quiet	quietly
honest	honestly	slow	slowly
interesting	interestingly	strong	strongly
late	lately		

Spelling Rules for Adverbs

	Adjectives	Adverbs
1. After most adjectives, add -ly.	accidental interesting nice peaceful	accidentally interestingly nicely peacefully
2. After -y, delete y and add -ily.	easy happy	easily happily
3. After -ic, add -ally.	automatic terrific	automatically terrifically
4. After a consonant + -le, drop the e and add -y.	gentle terrible	gently terribly

16. Modal Verbs and Modal-like Expressions

Modals are helper verbs. Most modals have multiple meanings.

Function	Modal Verb	Time	Example
Ability	can	present	I **can** speak three languages.
	could	past	She **couldn't** attend class yesterday.
	be able to	present, past	I**'m not able** to help you tomorrow.
	know how to	present, past	I **know how to** speak two languages.
Possibility	can	present	I **can** meet you at 3:00 for coffee.
	could	past	People **could** read the newspaper online many years ago.
Requests less formal	can	present, future	**Can** you stop that noise now?
more formal	could would	present, future	**Could** you turn off your cell phone, please? **Would** you please come to my party?
Permission less formal	can could	present, future	You **can** give me your answer next week. Yes, you **could** watch TV now.
more formal	may	present, future	You **may** leave now.
Advice	should ought to might want to	present, future	What **should** you do if you live in a noisy place? You really **ought to** save your money. You **might want to** wait until next month.
Suggestions	Why don't Let's	present, future	**Why don't** we study together? **Let's** read the chapter together.
Necessity	have to need to must	past, present, future	We **had to** cancel our date at the last minute. She **needs to** make a schedule. All students **must** send their applications out on time.
Conclusion	must	present, future	Today is Monday, so tomorrow **must** be Tuesday.

17. Stative (Non-Action) Verbs

1. Stative verbs describe states, not actions.

These are stative verbs: *love, know, want, need, seem, mean,* and *agree.*

Use the simple present with stative verbs, not the present progressive.

*I **don't like** rude people.* NOT *~~I'm not liking~~ rude people.*

*What **do** you **know** about this?* NOT *What ~~are you knowing~~?*

*They **seem** upset.* NOT *They ~~are seeming~~ upset.*

*Experts **don't agree** on the meaning of some gestures.*

NOT *Experts ~~are not agreeing~~ on the meaning of some gestures.*

2. Some verbs have a stative meaning and an action meaning.

STATIVE	*I **think** grammar is fun.* (= an opinion)	ACTION	*I'm **thinking** about my homework.* (= using my mind)
STATIVE	*The book **looks** interesting.* (= appears)	ACTION	*We're **looking** at the book right now.* (= using our eyes) appears)
STATIVE	*Do you **have** a dog?* (= own)	ACTION	*Are you **having** a good time?* (= experiencing)

3. You can use *feel* with the same meaning in the simple present and the present progressive.

*I **feel** tired today.*   OR   *I'm **feeling** tired today.*

*How **do** you **feel**?*   OR   *How **are** you **feeling**?*

18. Verbs + Gerunds and Infinitives

Verbs Followed by a Gerund Only	
admit	keep (= continue)
avoid	mind (= object to)
consider	miss
delay	postpone
deny	practice
discuss	quit
enjoy	recall (= remember)
finish	risk
imagine	suggest
involve	understand

Verbs Followed by an Infinitive Only		
afford	help	pretend
agree	hope	promise
arrange	intend	refuse
attempt	learn	seem
decide	manage	tend (= be likely)
deserve	need	threaten
expect	offer	volunteer
fail	plan	want
forget	prepare	

Verbs Followed by a Gerund or an Infinitive		
begin	like	start
continue	love	
hate	prefer	

19. Academic Word List (AWL) Words and Definitions

Academic Word	Definition
academic (adj) [U1] [U22]	relating to schools, especially colleges and universities
adult (n) [U11]	person who has grown to his or her full size and strength; not a child
affect (v) [U16]	have an influence on someone or something
analyst (n) [U18]	someone who studies or examines something in detail, such as finances, computer systems, or the economy
appropriate (adj) [U30]	correct or right for a particular situation
area (n) [U7] [U8] [U33]	specific part of a country, city, town, etc.
assignment (n) [U28]	specific job or responsibility that someone gives you
available (adj) [U30]	ready to use or get, such as an apartment or a parking space
challenge (n) [U16]	something that requires a lot of mental or physical effort
chapter (n) [U29]	separate part of a book that divides it into sections
comment (n) [U7] [U21]	an opinion or remark
communicate (v) [U21] [U23]	give messages or information to others through speech, writing, body movements, or signals
communication (n) [U23] [U29] [U32]	way of sending messages or information to others through speaking, writing, using body movement, or sending signals
community (n) [U5] [U14]	the people who live in a particular area; also a neighborhood
computer (n) [U1] [U2] [U14] [U26] [U28] [U32]	an electronic device that can store large amounts of information
concentrate (v) [U29]	direct your attention and thought to an activity or subject
concept (n) [U13]	idea
conference (n) [U4]	large formal meeting
contact (v) [U5] (n) [U17] [U23] [U31]	communicate with someone
contract (n) [U12]	written legal agreement
corporation (n) [U32]	large company
create (v) [U11] [U25] [U30]	make something new or imaginative
credit (n) [U15]	method of buying items or services and paying for them in the future
crucial (adj) [U23]	extremely important
culture (n) [U7] [U23] [U27]	the way of life of a particular people
definitely (adv) [U29]	without doubt, certainly
design (n) [U26] [U27]	the details or features of a picture or building
designer (n) [U27]	person who imagines how to make something and creates a plan for it
distribute (v) [U13]	give something to many people
economy (n) [U18]	the system of trade and industry in a city, region, or country

Academic Word	Definition
editor (n) [U27]	person who corrects and makes changes to texts, such as books or magazines
eventually (adv) [U14]	happening at a later time
expand (v) [U13]	make something bigger
expert (n) [U23]	person with a high level of knowledge or skill about a particular subject
export (v) [U17] (n) [U33]	send items to another country for sale or use
feature (n) [U3] [U11]	an important characteristic
fee (n) [U15]	money you pay for a service
file (n) [U3]	collection of information in a computer stored as one unit with one name
finally (adv) [U12] [U16] [U18] [U27]	at the end or after some delay
financial (adj) [U22]	relating to money
focus (v) [U29]	direct attention toward something or someone
foundation (n) [U9]	organization that provides financial support for activities and groups
global (adj) [U32]	relating to the whole world
goal (n) [U5] [U22] [U29]	purpose, something you want to achieve
grade (n) [U29]	measure of the quality of a student's schoolwork
grant (n) [U30]	sum of money that a university, government, or an organization gives to someone for a purpose, such as to do research or study
intelligent (adj) [U14]	able to understand and learn well; for example, an intelligent person
issues (n) [U22]	current subjects or problems that people are talking about, such as climate change, terrorism, etc.
job (n) [U5] [U18] [U20] [U22] [U27] [U28]	regular work that a person does to earn money
link (n) [U5]	word or image on a website that can take you to another document or website
major (n) [U1] [U22] [U27] [U29]	the main subject that a college student is studying
networking (n) [U5] [U21] [U26]	the process of meeting and talking to people who might be useful to know, especially in your job
persistent (adj) [U30]	having the ability to continue doing something even when there are difficulties
physical (adj) [U19]	relating to the body
positive (adj) [U23] [U31]	happy or hopeful
processed (adj) [U25]	treated with chemicals that preserve or give food extra taste or color
professional (n) [U5]	person who does work that needs special training
promote (v) [U25]	encourage or support something

Academic Word	Definition
publishing (n) [U27]	the business of making books, magazines, and newspapers
region (n) [U10]	particular area or part of a state, country, or the earth's surface
relax (v) [U8] [U31]	become calm and comfortable, and not worried
research (n) [U16] [U29]	the study of a subject in order to discover information
researcher (n) [U8] [U16] [U24]	person who studies something to learn detailed information about it
respond (v) [U18]	answer in words or actions
schedule (n) [U3] [U11] [U25] [U30]	list of planned activities or things to do at a certain time
site (n) [U5] [U21] [U26]	place
specific (adj) [U30]	relating to one thing and not others
stable (adj) [U18]	safe, not likely to change
stressed (adj) [U8] [U11] [U30]	very nervous or worried
survey (n) [U9]	set of questions to find out people's habits or beliefs about something
symbolize (v) [U10]	use a sign or mark to represent something
task (n) [U11] [U29]	small job or something you have to do
team (n) [U4]	number of people who act together as a group, such as a sports team
technology (n) [U21] [U32]	the different ways we use scientific discoveries for a practical purpose, such as a computer or cell phone
text (v) [U3] [U21] [U29]	send messages through a cell phone
topic (n) [U10] [U21]	subject or theme
tradition (n) [U10]	something that has existed for a long time in a culture, such as beliefs, stories, and songs
traditional (adj) [U7]	existing for a long time
vary (v) [U23]	change or cause to be different
virtual (adj) [U28]	describes a set of images or sounds a computer can make to represent a real place or situation, such as a virtual classroom
volunteer (adj) [U8] [U14]	consisting of people who work without receiving money

20. Pronunciation Table International Phonetic Alphabet (IPA)

Vowels	
Key Words	**International Phonetic Alphabet**
cake, mail, pay	/eɪ/
pan, bat, hand	/æ/
tea, feet, key	/iː/
ten, well, red	/e/
ice, pie, night	/aɪ/
is, fish, will	/ɪ/
cone, road, know	/oʊ/
top, rock, stop	/ɑ/
blue, school, new, cube, few	/uː/
cup, us, love	/ʌ/
house, our, cow	/aʊ/
saw, talk, applause	/ɔː/
boy, coin, join	/ɔɪ/
put, book, woman	/ʊ/
alone, open, pencil, atom, ketchup	/ə/

Consonants

Key Words	International Phonetic Alphabet
bid, jo**b**	/b/
do, fee**d**	/d/
food, sa**f**e	/f/
go, do**g**	/g/
home, be**h**ind	/h/
kiss, ba**ck**	/k/
load, poo**l**	/l/
man, plu**m**	/m/
need, ope**n**	/n/
pen, ho**p**e	/p/
road, ca**r**d	/r/
see, re**c**ent	/s/
show, na**ti**on	/ʃ/
team, mee**t**	/t/
choose, wa**tch**	/tʃ/
think, bo**th**	/θ/
this, fa**th**er	/ð/
visit, sa**v**e	/v/
watch, a**w**ay	/w/
yes, on**i**on	/j/
zoo, the**s**e	/z/
bei**g**e, mea**s**ure	/ʒ/
jump, bri**dg**e	/dʒ/

Glossary of Grammar Terms

action verb a verb that describes an action.

  I **eat** breakfast every day.

  The band **played** in clubs every week.

adjective a word that describes or modifies a noun.

  That's a **beautiful** hat.

adverb a word that describes or modifies a verb, another adverb, or an adjective. Adverbs often end in -ly.

  Please drive **carefully**.

adverb of manner an adverb that describes how an action happens.

  I studied **hard** for our English test.

article the words a / an and the. An article introduces or identifies a noun.

  I bought **a** new MP3 player. **The** price was reasonable.

auxiliary verb (helping verb) a verb that comes before a main verb in a sentence. Modals are one kind of auxiliary verb. Do, have, and be can act as auxiliary verbs.

  Does he want to go to the library later?   The package **will** arrive today.

base form of the verb the form of a verb without any endings (-s or -ed) or to.

  come   go   take

clause a group of words that has a subject and a verb.

   SUBJECT   VERB

  My husband works every day.

comparative the form of an adjective or adverb that shows how two people, places, or things are different.

  My daughter is **older than** my son. (adjective)

  She does her work **more quickly** than he does. (adverb)

conjunction the words and, but, and or. They connect single words, phrases, or clauses.

  I bought my groceries **and** went home.

consonant a sound represented in writing by these letters of the alphabet: **b, c, d, f, g, h, j, k, l, m, n, p, q, r, s, t, v, w, x, y,** and **z.**

count noun a noun that you can count. Count nouns have a plural form.

  There are three **banks** on Oak Street.

definite article the is a definite article. Use the with a person, place, or thing that is familiar to you and your listener. Also, use the when the noun is unique – there is only one (the sun, the moon, the Internet).

  The movie we saw last week was very good.

  The moon and the stars were beautiful last night.

G1

demonstrative a word that "points to" things and people. The demonstratives are *this, that, these,* and *those.*

This is my English book. *That* one is yours.

determiner a word that comes before a noun to limit its meaning in some way. Some common determiners are *some, any, this, that, these, those, a, an, the, much,* and *many.* Possessive adjectives – *my, your, his, her, our, their* – are also determiners.

These computers have *many* parts.

Please give me *my* book.

formal language a style of writing you use when you don't know the other person very well or where it is not appropriate to show familiarity, such as in a business, a job interview, speaking to a stranger, or speaking to an older person who you respect.

Good evening. I'd like to speak with Ms. Smith. Is she available?

future a verb form that describes a time that hasn't come yet. In English, we express the future with *will, be going to,* and the present.

I*'ll meet* you tomorrow.

I*'m going to visit* my uncle and aunt next weekend.

We*'re taking* the test tomorrow.

gerund the base form of a verb + *-ing,* for example, *going, watching, working.* Gerunds follow some verbs or can act as the subject of a sentence.

She enjoyed *making* things.   Salsa *dancing* is a lot of fun.

helping verb see **auxiliary verb**.

imperative a type of clause that tells people to do something. It gives instructions, directions to a place, or advice. It usually starts with the base form of a verb. The negative form begins with *Don't.*

Listen to the conversation.

Don't open your books.

indefinite article *a/an* are the indefinite articles. Use *a/an* with a singular person, place, or thing when you and your listener are not familiar with it, or when the specific name of it is not important. Use *a* with consonant sounds. Use *an* with vowel sounds.

She's going to see *a* doctor today.   I had *an* egg for breakfast.

indefinite pronoun a pronoun that refers to people or things that are not specific, not known, or not the focus of the sentence. *Something, anything, nothing, somebody, anybody, someone,* and *anyone* are indefinite pronouns.

Everyone knows fruit is good for you.   Does *anybody* want dessert?

infinitive *to* + the base form of a verb.

I need *to get* home early tonight.

informal language a style of speaking or writing to friends, family, and children.

Hey, there. Nice to see you again.

information question (also called *Wh-* question) a question that begins with a *wh*-word (*who, what, when, where, why, how*). To answer this type of question, you need to provide information rather than answer *yes* or *no.*

Where were you yesterday?

How much does that cost?

irregular adjective an adjective that does not change its form in the usual way. For example, you do not make the comparative form by adding -er.

good → better

irregular adverb an adverb that does not change its form in the usual way. For example, you do not make the comparative form by adding -er.

badly → worse

irregular verb a verb that does not change its form in the usual way. For example, it does not form the simple past with -d or -ed. It has its own special form.

go → went   ride → rode   hit → hit

linking verb a verb that links the subject with an adjective. Linking verbs are *be, get, seem, look, feel, sound, smell,* and *taste.*

That coffee **smells good**.

main clause a clause that can be used alone as a complete sentence.

While he was working, **he discovered the cure**.

main verb a verb that functions alone in a sentence or with an auxiliary verb.

They **had** a meeting last week.

They **didn't have** many meetings this month.

measurement word a word or phrase that shows the amount of something. Measurement words can be singular or plural.

I bought **a box** of cereal, and Sonia bought **five pounds** of apples.

modal a verb such as *can, could, be able to, know how to, would, may, should, ought to, might want to, have to, need to,* and *must.* Modals modify the main verb to show ability, possibility, requests, permission, suggestions, advice, necessity, or obligation.

It **might** rain later today.

You **should** study harder if you want to pass this course.

non-action verb see **stative verb**.

noncount noun a noun that you cannot count. Noncount nouns use a singular verb and do not have a plural form.

Fish is good for you.

noun a word for a person, place, or thing. There are common nouns and proper nouns.

COMMON NOUN   PROPER NOUN

I stayed in a **hotel** on my trip to New York.   I stayed at the **Pennsylvania Hotel**.

object the person or thing that receives the action of the verb.

I remember **James**.

object pronoun a word that replaces a noun in the object position. Object pronouns are *me, you, him, her, it, us,* and *them.*

Sara loves exercise classes. She takes **them** three times a week.

past progressive a verb form that describes events in progress at a time in the past. The emphasis is on the action.

They **were watching** TV until late last night.

plural noun a noun that refers to more than one person, place, or thing.

students   women   roads

possessive a word that shows that someone owns or has something. The word can be an adjective, a noun, or a pronoun.

A: *Is this **Diane's** desk?*

B: *No, it's **my** desk. **Her** desk is in the other office. **Her boss's** desk is in that office, too.*

possessive determiner *my, your, his, her, its, our,* and *their* are words that can come before a noun to show possession.

possessive pronoun a word that tells who owns something. Possessive pronouns are *mine, yours, his, hers, ours,* and *theirs.*

*That coffee is **mine**. (mine = my coffee)*   *I think this one is **yours**. (yours = your coffee)*

preposition a word such as *above, at, below, for, in, next to, on, to,* or *with* that goes before a noun or pronoun to show location, time, or direction.

*The shoes are **under** the bed.*   *I'll see you **on** July 1.*   *The man is **in front of** the bakery.*

prepositional phrase a phrase that begins with a preposition; a noun or noun phrase follows the preposition.

*Class starts **in five minutes**.*

present progressive a verb form that describes an action or situation that is in progress now or around the present time. It is also used to indicate the near future.

*What **are** you **doing** right now?*

*I'**m leaving** for Spain next week.*

pronoun a word that replaces a noun or noun phrase. Some examples are *I, you, we, him, hers,* and *it.*

proper noun a noun that is the name of a specific person, place, or thing. It begins with a capital letter.

***Central Park** is in **New York City**.*

punctuation mark a symbol used in writing, such as a period (.), a comma (,), a question mark (?), or an exclamation point (!).

quantifier a word that tells the amount of something, such as *some, any, a lot of, a little, a few, much,* and *many.* Quantifiers can refer to large or small amounts.

*"Do we have **any** eggs?"*   *"Yes, I think we have **some**."*

regular verb a verb that changes its form in the usual way.

live ➞ live**s**

wash ➞ wash**ed**

sentence a complete thought or idea that has a subject and a main verb. In writing, it begins with a capital letter and has a punctuation mark at the end (. ? !). In an imperative sentence, the subject (you) is not usually stated.

This sentence is a complete thought.   *Turn to page 168 in your books.*

simple past a verb form that describes completed actions or events in the past.

*They **grew up** in Washington, D.C.*

*They **attended** Howard University and **graduated** in 2011.*

simple present a verb form that describes things that regularly happen, such as habits and routines (usual and regular activities). It also describes facts and general truths.

*I **play** games online every night.* (routine)

*They **have** many friends.* (fact)

singular noun a noun that refers to one person, place, or thing.

*He is my best **friend**.*

statement a sentence that gives information. It can be spoken or written.

Today is Thursday.

stative (non-action) verb a verb that describes a state or situation, not an action. It is usually in the simple present or simple past.

*I **remember** your friend.*

subject the person, place, or thing that performs the action of the verb.

***People** should eat lots of fruit and vegetables.*

subject pronoun a pronoun that replaces a noun in the subject position. Subject pronouns are *I, you, he, she, it, we,* and *they.*

***We** (Sara and I) are taking exercise classes.*

superlative the form of an adjective or adverb that compares one person, place, or thing to others in a group.

*The **most important** day is tomorrow.* (adjective)

*Who arrives **the earliest** at school every day?* (adverb)

third-person singular refers to *he, she,* and *it,* or a singular noun. In the simple present, the third-person singular form ends in *-s* or *-es.*

***It looks** warm and sunny today.*   ***He washes** the laundry on Saturdays.*

time clause a clause that shows the order of events and begins with a time word such as *when, before, after,* or *while.*

*I met Joanna **when I was living in Houston**.*

verb a word that describes the action or state of a subject.

*Alex **wears** jeans and a T-shirt to school.*

vowel a sound represented in writing by these letters of the alphabet: ***a, e, i, o,*** and ***u.***

Wh- question see **information question**.

***Yes / No* question** a question that begins with a form of *be* or an auxiliary verb. You can answer this question with *yes* or *no.*

*"**Are** they going to the movies?"*   *"**No**, they're not."*

*"**Can** you give me some help?"*   *"**Yes**, I can."*

Index

Art Credits

Illustration

Pat Byrnes: 10, 11, 43, 92, 106, 202 *(bottom)*, 236, 255, 269, 278, 290, 291, 308, 354, 356, 381, 392, 393; **Ed Fotheringham:** 21, 70, 328, 379;
Ben Hasler: 6, 7, 14, 63, 64, 146, 165, 206, 243, 274, 286, 314, 367;
Michael Mantel: 202 *(top)*, 296, 302; **Maria Rabinky:** 10, 66, 245, 403;
Monika Roe: 2, 18, 38, 62, 93, 128, 164, 198, 214, 242, 259, 268, 282, 298, 305, 310, 330, 348, 353, 368, 391; **Rob Schuster:** 26, 28, 180, 188, 189, 229; **Richard Williams:** 42, 65, 105, 174, 175, 219, 260, 281, 303, 304, 318, 340, 355, 394

Photography

5 ©Peter Cade/Getty Images; 9 *(left to right)* ©Jacqueline Veissid/Getty Images; ©Alamy; 19 ©Media Bakery; 31 ©Yellow Dog Productions Inc./Getty Images; 32 *(clockwise from top left)* ©Alamy; ©Istock Photos; ©Superstock; ©Andersen Ross/Getty Images; ©Alamy; ©Getty Images; ©Age Fotostock; 35 ©Sean Justice/Getty Images; 36 ©Keren Su/Getty Images; 46 ©Alamy; 47 ©Shutterstock; 48 *(left to right)* ©Media Bakery; ©Getty Images; ©Moodboard/ Getty Images; 52 ©Shutterstock; 58 ©Media Bakery; 60 *(both)* ©Media Bakery; 61 ©Media Bakery; 69 ©Cheryl Clegg Photography; 76 *(all)* ©Alamy; 79 ©Wendy Connett/Getty Images; 81 *(clockwise from top left)* ©Media Bakery; ©Shutterstock; ©Tom Brosnahan; 82 *(top to bottom)* ©Photo Library; ©Alamy; 86 ©Media Bakery; 88 *(both)* ©Alamy; 98 *(left to right)* ©Media Bakery; ©Alamy; ©Media Bakery; 99 ©Alamy; 102 *(top to bottom)* ©Howard Berman/ Getty Images; ©White Packert/Getty Images; 107 ©Absodels/Getty Images; 110 ©Alamy; 113 *(left to right)* ©Pontino/Alamy; ©Alamy; ©Media Bakery; 115 *(left to right)* ©Eric Fowke/Alamy; ©Michael Dwyer/Alamy; ©Jerry Driendl/ Getty Images; 122 ©Shutterstock; 126 ©Media Bakery; 131 ©Shutterstock; 133 ©Media Bakery; 134 ©Shutterstock; 137 ©NY Daily News/Getty Images; 138 *(top to bottom)* ©World History Archive/Alamy; ©Pat Gaines/Getty Images; 140 *(left to right)* Istock Photos; ©Lebrecht Music and Arts Photo Library/ Alamy; 144 *(left to right)* ©FPG/Getty Images; ©Jeremy Sutton-Hibbert/Alamy; ©Pictorial Press Ltd/Alamy; ©Classic Image/Alamy; 145 ©Alamy; 148 ©John M. Heller/Getty Images; 150 ©Media Bakery; 154 ©Courtesy of Pinkberry; 155 ©Courtesy of Pinkberry; 158 ©Stefan Kiefer/Vario Images/Alamy; 160 ©Everett Collection Inc/Alamy; 161 *(top to bottom)* ©Red Carpet Press/Alamy; ©Everett Collection Inc/Alamy; 167 ©Jeff Fusco/Getty Images; 168 ©Getty Images; 170 ©Media Bakery; 171 *(left to right)* ©Media Bakery; ©Shutterstock; 185 *(top to bottom)* ©Media Bakery; ©Johnny Greig/Alamy; ©Getty Images; 186 *(top to bottom)* ©Shutterstock; ©Shutterstock; ©Shutterstock; ©James Jackson/ Alamy; 190 ©Shutterstock; 191 *(all)* ©Shutterstock; 194 ©Andrew Twort/ Alamy; 197 *(top to bottom)* ©Media Bakery; ©Shutterstock; ©Shutterstock; 203 ©Robert Daemmrich/Getty Images; 210 ©Media Bakery; 213 ©AbleStock/ Thinkstock; 215 ©Getty Images; 216 ©Media Bakery; 218 ©Alamy; 220 *(left to right)* ©Larry Lilac/Alamy; ©Shutterstock; 224 *(top to bottom)* ©Robert Harding Picture Library Ltd/Alamy; ©Susan Marie Andersson/Getty Images; ©Gastromedia/Alamy; 228 *(top to bottom)* ©Danita Delimont/Alamy; ©David Gee/Alamy ©David Hanson/Getty Images; 230 *(top to bottom)* ©Dirk Freder/ Getty Images; ©Alamy; 233 *(top to bottom)* Media Bakery; ©Kathrin Ziegler/ Getty Images; 238 ©Media Bakery 241 ©Blend Images/Alamy; 246 *(top to bottom)* ©Octavio Campos Salles/Alamy; ©John W Banagan/Getty Images; 248 ©Tony Peacock/Alamy; 250 ©MBI/Alamy; 253 ©Hola Images/Getty Images; 264 ©Angela Hampton Picture Library/Alamy; 271 *(left to right)* ©Andres Rodriguez/Alamy; ©Alamy; ©Media Bakery; ©William King/Getty Images; 273 ©Media Bakery; 283 ©Photo Alto/Alamy; 294 ©Tom Mc Nemar/Alamy; 311 ©Burke/Triolo Productions/Getty Images; 316 *(both)* ©Media Bakery; 320 ©Courtesy of Ashley Qualls; 323 ©Media Bakery; 324 ©Somos Images/Alamy; 328 ©Getty Images; 334 ©Media Bakery; 338 *(left to right)* ©Picture Partners/ Photo Library; ©Ulrike Preuss/Photo Library; ©Echo/Getty Images; 339 *(top to bottom)* ©Alan Copson/Getty Images; ©Media Bakery; 343 *(top to bottom)* ©Angelo Hornak/Alamy; ©Frances Roberts/Alamy; 351 ©Photo Alto/Alamy; 360 ©UpperCut Images/Alamy; 364 ©Media Bakery; 367 ©Alamy; 372 ©Blend Images/Alamy; 376 ©Thomas Barwick/Getty Images; 378 ©Getty Images; 384 ©Media Bakery; 387 ©Media Bakery; 388 *(top to bottom)* ©Radius Images/ Alamy; ©QxQ Images/Datacraft/Getty Images; 398 *(top to bottom)* ©Media Bakery; ©Getty Images; 402 *(left to right)* ©Alamy; ©Adrian Lyon/Alamy; 412 *(clockwise from top left)* ©Antony Giblin/Getty Images; ©Robert Harding/Getty Images; ©Nik Wheeler/Alamy; ©Jon Arnold Images Ltd/Alamy; 416 ©TAO Images Limited/Alamy; 418 ©RubberBall/Alamy; 423 *(all)* ©Alamy